The U.S. Declaration of Independence for Everyone

The U.S. Declaration of Independence for Everyone

Jerome Agel & Mort Gerberg

A Perigee Book

157 0947 - 354

A Perigee Book
Published by The Berkley Publishing Group
A division of Penguin Putnam Inc.
375 Hudson Street
New York, New York 10014

First edition: June 2001
Published simultaneously in Canada.

The Penguin Putnam Inc. World Wide Web site address is
www.penguinputnam.com

Library of Congress Cataloging-in-Publication Data

Agel, Jerome.
    The U.S. Declaration of Independence for everyone / Jerome Agel, Mort Gerberg.
        p.   cm.
    ISBN 0-399-52698-6
    1. United States. Declaration of Independence.   2. United States—Politics and
government—1775–1783.   I. Title: United States Declaration of Independence
for everyone.   II. Gerberg, Mort.   III. Title.

E221 .A47 2001
973.3'13—dc21
                                                                                    00-140071

Printed in the United States of America

10   9   8   7   6   5   4   3   2   1

JAN 14 2002

The U.S. Declaration of Independence for Everyone

A Deadly Family Quarrel

We hold these truths to be self-evident, that all men are created equal, that they are endowed by their Creator with certain unalienable Rights. That among these are Life, Liberty and the pursuit of Happiness. That to secure these rights, Governments are instituted among Men, deriving their just powers from the consent of the governed.

In the course of human events in the year 1776—nearly eight centuries after Vikings first settled in North America, nearly three centuries after Columbus made the first of four voyages across the ocean blue and into the Caribbean Sea—Great Britain's ethnically and naturally diverse thirteen colonies along the North Atlantic Seaboard* and beyond the Alleghenies of the "new world" in General Congress, Assembled, agreed that Great Britain's mulish George III, king since 1760, was a traitor to the people of the thirteen colonies—his people! The monarch, in fact, had been making war on the Americans for more than a year with the most powerful military force in the world.

The colonies, accustomed to control of their own lives, voted to dissolve the political bands that connected them with Britain, the "Mother Country," and to "assume among the powers of the earth, the separate and equal station to which the Laws of Nature and of Nature's God entitle them."

For 169 years, blood and English had linked Britain and its faraway

---

*New Hampshire, Massachusetts-Bay, Rhode Island, Connecticut, New Jersey, Georgia, Virginia, Maryland, New York, Pennsylvania, Delaware, North Carolina, South Carolina. Population of the 13 colonies: about 2.5-million.

American colonies. Most of the colonists were descendants of Britons; they thought of themselves as English, they thought of themselves as fellow subjects. However, the Americans did not have representatives in the British Parliament, yet they were bound by its edicts. The continent was subject to an external power; Britain wanted increased revenue from the colonies.

American patriotism didn't manifest itself until Britain infringed on what the colonists considered their rights. Not even the war, which was being waged since deadly skirmishes between British troops and the Massachusetts militia in the Massachusetts villages of Lexington and Concord in April 1775 had provoked a rupture. Reconciliation was still a possibility.

"TYRANT"

The Stamp Act of 1765 had roused a wave of unrest. Colonists refused to pay a tax on purchases of legal and commercial paper. It was the first direct tax that Parliament had imposed on the Americans, who insisted they could be taxed only by representatives they had chosen: taxation with representation.

A newly formed radical society, Sons of Liberty, rioted in the streets against British restrictions. There were vigorous chapters in New York and Boston. Paul Revere, the patriotic Bostonian, was a courier.

Charles Townshend, Chancellor of Britain's Exchequer, stirred deep resentment with the imposition of still another restriction. In an attempt to raise revenue, the Townshend Act of 1767 levied duties on glass, lead, paint, paper, and tea imports to America. Three years later, redcoats fired on an unruly mob in Boston, in what became known as the "Boston Massacre."

British legislation labeled Intolerable Acts by the colonists followed the Boston Tea Party (1773) on three tea-carrying ships. The British replied to destruction of the tea by patriots disguised as Indians by shutting down the port of Boston, prohibiting town meetings in Massachusetts, and compelling both the quartering of soldiers in colonial homes and the trying in England of colonial officials accused of crimes committed while enforcing British laws.

Americans continued to protest British control. The alarm bell of revolution was beginning to clang: "To these grievous acts and measures Americans cannot submit, but . . . hope that their fellow subjects in Great Britain will, on a revision of them, restore us to that state in which both countries found happiness and prosperity."

In December 1775, Britain rolled out its mightiest cannon: The Prohibition Act forbid commerce with the American colonies.

The colonies came to believe that any obligation of allegiance had ended. Patriotic local assemblies evolved into the First Continental Congress. Fifty-six delegates, representing every colony except Georgia, looked for a remedy from England's oppression, both commercial and political. The colonies did not consider independence. They wanted the British government to recognize their rights. British actions were challenging the very existence of provincial government.

Emigration and a vibrant secular life had reshaped the colonial population into a powerful consuming society. The American people were on the cusp of the first modern revolution in the postmodern society. After "Lexington and Concord," where illegal arms had been stored, the two sides flailed at each other all over the map, for 1300 miles, from Massachusetts-Bay's rocky Maine coast in the north to Georgia's sandy hills in the far south. On land and at sea, the American Revolution was under way.

Britain was a behemoth in the western hemisphere. It had a foothold in Canada; it had acquired Nova Scotia in 1717, captured Quebec in 1759, and took control of the rest of Canada in 1763. Many Americans, calling themselves United Empire Loyalists, moved out of the colonies northward to Canada.

The matchless phrase "a decent respect to the opinions of mankind" required that the exasperated Americans declare to "a candid world" the causes that propelled them inexorably to the inevitable.

To justify revolution and independence, the colonists lodged a throng of grievances against the monarch. Facts "submitted to a candid world" indicted King George III for treason against his American subjects.

One of the most pointed complaints: "declaring us out of his Protection and waging War against us."

Thomas Jefferson asserted, "We want neither inducement nor power to declare and assert a separation. It is will, alone, that is wanting and that is growing apace under the fostering hand of our king."

Congress wanted more than twenty "injuries and usurpations" quashed. The charge on slavery was said to be extravagantly worded.

The king's response for redress: taxation without representation would continue. John Adams, Benjamin Franklin, and other political theorists in the colonies argued that taxation without representation was unbridled abuse of power.

Some colonists favored reconciliation even more than independence. They wanted restoration of harmony. It's said they were willing to bleed at every vein in defense of the sovereign. But the desire for independence, John Adams noted, became "like a torrent."

Yet some Americans believed they would be worse off as an independent nation than they were under a hostile king and legislature.

England's interest in North America went back centuries. Daring English mariners, usually at their own expense, reconnoitered the unfamiliar Atlantic coastline. As early as 1498, the English flag had sailed along the New England shore, with John Cabot as navigator. In 1607, Englishmen established a substantial settlement at Jamestown, Virginia. In 1620, the *Mayflower* arrived at Cape Cod, Massachusetts, many of its passengers seeking religious freedom. England established colonies along the coast. In 1664, English troops (forces of the Duke of York) seized the Dutch colonial territory of New Netherland; New Amsterdam became New York City.

English sites developed their own characteristics; essentially, each site was self-governing; the first settlers did pretty much as they pleased. Centralized authority accelerated, especially in the area of trade.

England became eager for command of America's blooming economic life. After the French and Indian War (the American part of Europe's Seven Years' War: 1754–1763), the triumphant Crown, saddled with a huge war debt, wanted the colonies to help pay for their future defense.

England tightened control. Strict enforcement of Acts of trade and navigation augmented stress. The Acts eliminated foreign competition, allowing commercial benefits to accrue to England and the colonies, and demanded that the quartering of British soldiers be at local expense. Popular sentiment plus defiance of English law now contributed to the expanding urge for independence.

The outraged, especially New Englanders, had had their fill of King George III and the "family quarrel." The transatlantic gulf widened. The king wanted his army to crush the Americans. The mightiest fighting force in North American history sent General George Washington's amateur soldiers retreating through swamps and forests.

The king treated his American subjects like aliens. By the time that nearly fifty delegates from twelve of the thirteen colonies (New York was absent) convened as the Second Continental Congress in the red-brick city of Philadelphia, the largest city in the colonies (population: about 40,000; 90 percent of all colonists lived in the rural countryside), popular local sentiment was swinging away from reconciliation. When the monarch hired more than 12,000 Hessian mercenaries for his American war, independence no longer could be ignored.

As American Indian cultures disappeared or merged with other cultures, a jumble of peoples dominated the colonies: English and Germans and Dutch and Irish and Jews and Scots. English settlers constituted barely half of the population in New York, New Jersey, and Pennsylvania. But Germans constituted the largest European immigration group in colonial America. The English shipped as many as five thousand convicts to America between 1718 and 1776.

Petitions, notes, and boycotts drove the rebel movement. Congress—the greatest generation!—believed that insurrection would fail unless its goal was identified. The goal was independence from Great Britain. It'd been a year since "Lexington and Concord."

In mid-May of 1776, John Adams suggested that the Second Continental Congress urge the colonies to form new governments "where no government sufficient to the exigencies of their affairs had been hitherto established."

5

Less than a month later, an aristocratic Virginian delegate, Richard Henry Lee, offered a resolution that put Congress on the track for independence. Lee told Congress that, "These United Colonies are, and of right ought to be, free and independent States, that they are absolved from all allegiance to the British Crown, and that all political connections between them and the State of Great Britain is, and ought to be, totally dissolved. That it is expedient forthwith to take the most effectual measures for forming foreign alliances. That a plan of confederation be prepared and transmitted to the respective colonies for their consideration and approbation."

Nine colonies favored the fact of separation. Two, Pennsylvania and South Carolina, opposed it; New York's delegation abstained, awaiting instructions. Delaware was deadlocked. When New York came on board, the resolution was approved unanimously.

Congress, on the edge of declaring separation, appointed a committee of five to draft a declaration embodying the intention of delegate Lee's proposal: Thomas Jefferson (age 33), of Virginia; Benjamin Franklin (70), of Pennsylvania; Roger Sherman (55), of Connecticut; John Adams (40), of Massachusetts; and Robert L. Livingston (29), of New York. Adams believed that the revolution had already occurred in "the minds of the people."

Debates in Philadelphia went on behind closed doors and shut windows in the Pennsylvania State House. The ground-floor meeting room was steamy in the late spring.

Between June 11 and June 28, 1776, a late-arriving, six-foot, two-inch red-haired Virginia delegate, the freckled son of a planter, worked quickly at a self-designed, custom-made portable desk, or box, on the second floor of temporary lodgings in a new three-story house in Philadelphia. The delegate was taciturn and shy, 33-year-old patriot celebrated for his talent for felicitous composition. Thomas Jefferson was to compose an avowal of revolution, a public confession of treason. As nearly as possible, he would write an expression of the American mind. Legitimate power would be "just power."

(Jefferson believed that the tree of liberty must be refreshed from time to time with the blood of its patriots and tyrants: "It is its natural manure." He was devoted to revolution and extreme liberty.)

Three thousand miles to the east, on the other side of the Atlantic, the British monarch was urging the "most decisive exertions" to put an end to the rebellion. The freeborn Englishmen in America were jealous of their liberties. Town meetings fostered an independence of spirit. George broke the last tie.

Jefferson's facile pen, attacking the authority of the king and resisting Parliament, endowed the revolt with a philosophical foundation of human rights, though most of the document concerned despotic acts. Jefferson wanted to demonstrate that the king sought establishment of an absolute tyranny. (Previously, the colonists had directed their criticism against Parliament or the king's ministers, never against the king himself. Charging George with wrongdoing was a bold move.)

The Declaration, Jefferson asserted, was a "fundamental act of Union of these States. The principles of the instrument should be cherished in the bosom of our citizens." All monarchs were inherently evil.

Two committee members, the delegates John Adams and the bon vivant Benjamin Franklin, reviewed and revised Jefferson's draft. (Jefferson termed Adams "our Colossus on the floor.") Jefferson thought changes to be "mutilations." When Congress reviewed the draft paragraph by paragraph over three days, Jefferson sat nervously and silently by. Principles were polished. Some claims were cut back or aborted. Extreme or untenable assertions were expunged. The lengthy reference to slavery was removed, so that South Carolina, with many slaves, would support the "charter of freedom." John Adams defended the slavery change. (Elsewhere, reformers were campaining against slaveholding generally, and against planter cruelty particularly. Not all the northern states wished to condemn slavery. In the first U.S. Census, in 1797, nearly 700,000 of the fledgling republic were black slaves.)

Delegates added references to God. The issues of concern were taxes, troops, and tyranny. Richard Henry Lee, whose resolution had accelerated independence, also was distressed by the changes. "It is passing pitiful," he wrote, "that the rage for change should be so unhappily applied. However, the thing in its nature is so good that no cookery can spoil the dish for the palates of free men."

On June 28, 1776, the Committee of Five submitted to the Second Continental Congress "A Declaration by the Representatives of the United States of America, in General Assembled." On July 2, Congress decided in favor of independence, adopting Lee's resolution. Then it spent three days debating and amending the Jefferson manuscript, approving it on July 4. Delegates, "appealing to the Supreme Judge of the world for the

rectitude of our intention," voted unanimously for independence. (Franklin had observed that "every day furnishes us with new causes of increasing enmity.")

The Americans took up arms in the name of liberty. The Spirit of '76: Congress's Revolutionary Army captured Fort Ticonderoga and Crown Point, at Lake Champlain. Congress, breathing the air 'round Tom Paine, condemned George III, a "royal brute . . . the greatest enemy this continent hath" (Paine's description).

Paine's pamphlet *Common Sense* had created a rush of sentiment for independence among colonists previously loyal to the Crown. *Common Sense* was a loud, clear call for independence. It was a turning point. Paine believed that not a place upon Earth "might be so happy as America. Her situation is remote from all the wrangling world, and she has nothing to do but to trade with them."

Congress wanted a society in which people could flourish. The Declaration of Independence, incisive and powerful, declared the fundamental act of Union and the fundamental premises of American nationhood: "Governments are instituted among Men, deriving their just powers from the consent of the governed."

The Declaration stated the colonies' reason for leaving the imperial embrace. It asserted the fundamental American idea of government based on the theory of Natural Rights. It indicted King George for willfully infringing those rights in order to establish an absolute tyranny over the colonies.

Between 1680 and 1763, the British had fought four major wars involving American mainland colonies. America's War of Independence was yet another. The merciless British were thrown out of the South, but they forced General Washington out of Brooklyn.

On July 4, a 76-degree, rainy summer day in Philadelphia, Congress again met in the state house on Walnut Street. Again, the windows were closed, the room stuffy.

Congress authenticated the document, then ordered it engrossed on animal skin, or parchment, proclaimed, and distributed to the States. Charles Thomson, the Congressional secretary, read the document aloud, and confirmed the unanimous vote. Boston's adored John Hancock, president of the Congress, and one of the richest men in the colonies, signed the document, boldly. General Washington had it read to the troops.

Within a month, more and more members of the Second Continental Congress began putting their name to it; they knew they could be hanged for treason. (About a third of the population of the colonies remained loyal to the king.)

And so the united colonies left the British empire and became the

United States of America. Crowds greeted readings of the Declaration with huzzahs—loud ones.

It took three months for King George, isolated thousands of maritime miles away, to learn of the declaration. He told Parliament, "One great advantage will be derived from the object of the rebels being openly avowed. We shall have unanimity at home founded in the general conviction of the justice and necessity of our measure."

A British lord, however, praised the papers transmitted from America: "For singular moderation, manly spirits, sublime sentiments and simplicity of language, for everything respectable and honorable, the Congress of Philadelphia stand unrivaled. The histories of Greece and Rome give us nothing equal to it. And all attempts to impose servitude on such a mighty continental nation must be in vain. . . ."

But the English did not go quietly. Or quickly. America's War of Independence consumed five more years. The Declaration, however, inspired the rebel army.

General Washington strove to animate and encourage his men to noble actions: "The fact of unborn millions will depend, under God, on the courage and conduct of this army. Our cruel and unrelenting enemy leaves us no choice but a braver resistance or the most abject submission. This is all we can expect. We have therefore to resolve to conquer or die. Our own country's honor, all call upon us, for a vigorous and manly exertion, and if we now shamefully fail we shall become infamous to the whole world . . . Let us therefore animate and encourage each other, and show the whole world that a free man contending for liberty on his own ground is superior to any slavish mercenary on earth."

France's entry, allying with Washington's force, was a decisive factor in forcing the British to give up their American colonies.

The world turned upside down. The British, cornered on a peninsula at Yorktown, Virginia, raised the white flag in October 1781. But the redcoats hung on to New York City for another year. In the Treaty of Paris, signed in late 1783, the British recognized the political independence and territorial sovereignty of the United States of America.

It had been a long haul from colonial protests against the sugar tax and the Stamp Act. The United States became the world's only republic. All sects became united as well as all nations.

A few years later, "We the People"—white, male, principally Protestant, motivated (some say) by pocketbook patriotism—came to feel keenly that the instrument of government, the Articles of Confederation, framed by the "traitorous" Founding Fathers during the stress of the Revolutionary War, wasn't working. In 1787, they framed the Constitution, to this day the supreme laws of the land.

The Declaration of Independence—the engrossed Declaration was signed on August 2, 1776—became:

- "the defining event of a heroic age;"
- "the most sacred of all American political scriptures;"
- "one of the great political documents of the West;"
- "the most important of all American historical documents;"
- "America's birth certificate;"
- "the American symbol of independence, revolution, and liberty;"
- "the charter of freedom;"
- "a revolutionary manifesto;"
- "a summary of political thought;"
- "an experiment of supreme importance, with immortal principles;"
- "a holy writ;"
- "the basis of future governments."

Coincidentally, Thomas Jefferson and John Adams, both erstwhile presidents, died on the fiftieth anniversary of the Declaration, July 4, 1826. Abigail Adams had said that Jefferson was "the only person with whom my companion could associate with perfect freedom and reserve." Nearly four decades later, another U.S. chief executive, the sixteenth, Abraham Lincoln, declared that the Declaration had been a stirring call to throw off the bonds of tyranny. It was "the electric cord . . . that links the hearts of patriotic and liberty-loving men together." On his way to his first inauguration Lincoln had said, "I have never had a feeling politically that did not spring from the sentiments embodied in the Declaration of Independence."

The peregrinating Declaration has had many homes: Philadelphia, of course; New York City; Baltimore, Maryland; York, Pennsylvania; Princeton, New Jersey; Trenton, N.J.; Annapolis, Md., Leesburg, Virginia. The parchment was sheltered in the house of a clergyman in Leesburg during the British attack on the nation's capital in the War of 1812, and at Fort Knox, Kentucky, during the Second World War. (For three years, it had been in Jefferson's custody.)

Not until the 1840s was the document put on public display.

For thirty-five years, the Declaration hung on a wall, opposite a large window, exposed to the chill of winter and the glare and heat of summer, in the new Patent Office of the nation. During the centennial celebration, in 1876, it was exhibited in a fireproof safe, behind a plate-glass door, in Philadelphia. Signatures already were dim. It also has been displayed in the U.S. State Department and in the Library of Congress.

On July 8, 1776, the Declaration of Independence with its emphasis on rights in each individual's humanity was proclaimed in public for the first time at high noon, the Committee of Safety and Inspection of Philadelphia went to the state house, where the Declaration was read to a large number of inhabitants of the city and county. It was received with general applause and heartful satisfaction. In the evening, the late king's coat-of-arms was brought from the hall in the state house and burned amidst acclamation. The American Revolution still had thirteen years to go.

After Pearl Harbor (December 7, 1941), the Declaration was shipped under heavy guard—armed secret-service agents and troops of the thirteenth Armored Division—for safekeeping to Fort Knox, Kentucky, where the United States stores gold reserves. (The Constitution, another U.S. crown jewel, also was shipped to Fort Knox.) The cracking Declaration was repaired.

Eventually, the Declaration of Independence was placed in a helium-filled case enclosed in a wooden crate lain on a mattress in an armored Marine Corps personnel carrier. Escorted by ceremonial troops, two tanks, and four servicemen carrying submachine guns, the document was moved to the National Archives, in Washington, D.C. It is exhibited there today.

An original copy of the Declaration of Independence in Jefferson's own hand was exhibited in Paris's Bibliotheque Nationale. Housed in a big, nondescript suitcase, it had flown from New York in a window seat and was securely strapped in. When the copy, owned by the New York Public Library, is not on display, the document is kept in a secret spot that is *never* disclosed. *The New Yorker* magazine has reported that "during the Second World War, the library copy was shipped to the vaults of the Guarantee Trust Company in Saratoga Springs, New York— the idea, presumably, being that the Germans would not bomb a racetrack and a spa." One of the three extant copies of the Declaration was purchased for $7 million in 2000 by a long-time television-program producer. The copy is scheduled to be displayed around the United States for the first time since a copy toured the nation in the 1940s on the Freedom Train.

The First Continental Congress

Meeting in secret for about seven weeks (September 5–October 26, 1774), in Philadelphia's Carpenters Hall, the fifty-six patriotic delegates of the governing body of aggrieved American colonies demanded amends for accumulated grievances, especially for British measures taken against Massachusetts. Remote Georgia was not represented. George Washington appeared in uniform. Virginia's delegates were spirited. Congress voted a declaration of rights (life, liberty, property, assembly, trial by jury) and rejected a blend of colonial freedom. Delegates included Founding Fathers John Adams, Samuel Adams, and Patrick Henry. Congress agreed to meet again if King George III did not redress the grievances. Congress appointed Washington as commander-in-chief of the Continental armies but nobody urged independence. Congress coordinated the resistance of the newly formed states in the Revolutionary War, and won the support of foreign allies, especially France. The process was painful, America's birth would be bloody. Some Virginia militiamen painted "Liberty or Death" on their hunting shirts.

The Second Continental Congress

Facing financial woes, it met in the state house in Philadelphia on May 10, 1775 a month after "Lexington and Concord" "Phrensy of revenge." Congress had no right to levy taxes, and it received little or no money from colonies not in harm's way. Private citizens contributed much money in return for U.S. interest-bearing securities. The battle of Bunker Hill in Boston, occurred on June 17. At excessive cost the redcoats netted a nominal victory. The Constitutional Convention of 1787 gave the U.S. a strong central government for the first time in many years. Congress issued an immense volume of paper money or bills of credit in order to buy supplies and to compensate the soldiers. The Revolutionary War continued for five more years. In the summer and early autumn of 1781, Lord Charles Cornwallis's British army was cornered on Virginia's York-town peninsula. Except for the Peace Treaty, the Revolutionary War was over.

Grievances

The Second Continental Congress leveled a litany of grievances against King George III, for the first time making him—rather than others—the target of colonial objection. Thomas Jefferson asserted that "the history of the present king of Great Britain is a history of unremitting injuries and usurpations, all having in direct object the establishment of an absolute tyranny over these states. To prove this, let facts be submitted to the world 'for the truth of which we pledge a faith yet unsullied by falsehood'." The monarch was deemed a traitor to his people. Congress's grievances:

H

H • • • has refused to Assent to Laws, the most wholesome and necessary for the public good.

2. He has forbidden his Governors to pass laws of immediate and pressing importance, unless suspended in their operation till his Assent should be obtained; and when so suspended, he has utterly neglected to attend to them.

3. He has refused to pass other Laws for the accommodation of large districts of people, unless those people would relinquish the right of Representation in the Legislature, a right inestimable to them and formidable to tyrants only.

4. He has called together legislative bodies at places unusual, uncomfortable, and distant from the depository of their Public Records, for the sole purpose of fatiguing them into compliance with his measures.

5. He has dissolved Representative Houses repeatedly, for opposing with manly firmness his invasions on the rights of the people.

6. He has refused for a long time, after such dissolutions, to cause others to be elected; whereby the Legislative Powers, incapable of Annihilation, have returned to the People at large for their exercise; the State remaining in the mean time exposed to all the dangers of invasion from without, and convulsions within.

7. He has endeavored to prevent the population of these States; for that purpose obstructing the Laws for Naturalization of Foreigners; refusing to pass others to encourage their migration hither and raising the conditions of new Appropriations of Lands.

8. He has obstructed the Administration of Justice by refusing his Assent to Laws for establishing Judiciary Powers.

9. He has made Judges dependent on his Will alone, for the tenure of their offices, and the amount and payment of their salaries.

10. He has erected a multitude of New Offices, and sent hither swarms of Officers to harass our People, and eat out their substance.

11. He has kept among us, in times of peace, Standing Armies without the Consent of our legislatures.

12. He has affected to render the Military independent of and superior to the Civil Power.

13. He has combined with others to subject us to a jurisdiction foreign to our constitution, and unacknowledged by our laws; giving his Assent to their acts of pretended legislation.

14. For quartering large bodies of armed troops among us;

15. For protecting them, by a mock trial, from Punishment for any Murders which they should commit on the Inhabitants of these States;

16. For cutting off our Trade with all parts of the world;

17. For imposing taxes on us without our Consent;

18. For depriving us in many cases of Trial by Jury;

19. For transporting us beyond Seas to be tried for pretended offences;

20. For abolishing the free system of English Laws in a neighboring Province, establishing therein an Arbitrary government and enlarging its Boundaries so as to render it at once an example and fit instrument for introducing the same absolute rule into these colonies.

21. For taking away our Charters, abolishing our most valuable Laws, and altering fundamentally the Forms of our Governments;

22. For suspending our own Legislatures, & declaring themselves invested with Power to legislate for us in all cases whatsoever.

23. He has abdicated Government here, by declaring us out of his Protection, and urging War against us.

24. He has plundered our seas, ravaged our Coasts, burnt our towns, and destroyed the lives of our people.

25. He is at this time transporting large armies of foreign mercenaries to compleat the works of death, desolation & tyranny, already begun with circumstances of Cruelty & perfidy scarcely paralleled in the most barbarous ages, and totally unworthy the Head of a civilized nation.

26. He has constrained our fellow Citizens, taken Captive on the high Seas to bear Arms against their Country, to become the executioners of their friends & Brethren, or to fall themselves by their Hands.

27. He has endeavored to bring on the inhabitants of our frontiers, the merciless Indian Savages, whose known rule of warfare, is an undistinguished destruction of all ages, sexes, and conditions.

Two Expunged Grievances

Congress expunged two grievances, though "in every stage of these oppressions we have petitioned for redress in the most humble terms; our repeated petitions have been answered only by repeated injury, a price whose character is thus marked by every act which may define a tyrant, is unfit to be the ruler of a people (who mean to be free.)"

Removed was the charge that the king "has incited treasonable insurrections of our fellow citizens, with the allurements of forfeiture & confiscation of property." Also deleted was the charge concerning slavery. Southern delegates, especially South Carolina's, were unwilling to countenance any acknowledgement that slavery violated the most sacred right of life and liberty. The slavery passage had to be removed if endorsement of the proposed declaration was to be unanimous. The slavery charge had declared that King George III was waging "cruel war against human nature itself, violating its most sacred rights of life & liberty in the persons of a distant people, who never offended him, captivating and carrying them into slavery in another hemisphere, or to incur miserable death in their transportation thither. This piratical warfare, the opprobrium of *infidel* powers, is the warfare of the *Christian* king of Great Britain, determined to keep open a market where MEN should be bought & sold, he has prostituted his negative for suppressing every legislative attempt to prohibit or to restrain this execrable commerce: and that this assemblage of horrors might want no fact of distinguished die, he now is now exciting those very people to rise in arms among us, and to purchase that liberty of which *he* has deprived them, by murdering the people upon whom *he* also obtruded them: thus paying off former crimes committed against the *liberties* of one people, with crimes which he urge them to commit against the *lives* of another."

Paine: An Inspiration

Two years after emigrating from England to Philadelphia with letters of introduction from Benjamin Franklin, then a colonial agent in London, the political philosopher Thomas Paine (1737–1809) called for a break with Great Britain, his native land. Paine hated governments that rested on hereditary privilege. He declared that "The sun never shined on a cause (the American cause) more just. . . . Independence is the only Bond that can tye and keep us together."

Declaring that "my country is the world and my religion is to do good," Paine bolstered the morale of the American Revolutionary army with his periodical *Crisis*. (He also served in the army.) His forty-seven-page pamphlet called *Common Sense* sold upwards of half a million copies.

Paine believed that "if there ever was a just war, since the world began, it is this, in which America is now engaged." He believed that in a world "overrun with oppression" America would be "an asylum for mankind." A "thirst for absolute power is the natural disease of humanity."

Paine also believed: "Society in every state is a blessing, but

Government, even in its best state, is but a necessary evil; in its worst state, an intolerable one. . . . When we are planning for posterity, we ought to remember that virtue is not hereditary. . . . O! ye that love mankind! Ye that dare oppose not only the tyranny but the tyrant, stand forth! Every spot of the Old World is overrun with oppression. Freedom hath been hunted round the globe. Asia and Africa have long expelled her. Europe regards her as a stranger and England hath given her warning to depart. O! receive the fugitive and prepare in time an asylum for mankind." It was simply a matter of common sense that an island could not rule a continent.

Paine also wrote that: "The summer soldier and the sunshine patriot will, in this crisis, shrink from the service of his country; but he that stands it now, deserves the love and thanks of man and woman. Tyranny, like hell, is not easily conquered; yet we have this consolation with us, that the harder the conflict, the more glorious the triumph. What we obtain too cheap, we esteem too lightly; 'tis dearness only that gives everything its value. Heaven knows how to put a proper price upon its goods; and it would be strange indeed, if so celestial an article as Freedom should not be highly rated. Not a place upon earth might be so happy as America. Her situation is remote from all the wrangling world, and she has nothing to do but to trade with them. . . ."

At the turn of the century, John Adams hailed Paine: "I know not whether any man in the world has had more influence on its inhabitants or affairs for the last thirty years than Tom Paine."

Paine's observations, it's been noted, became part of the intellectual foundation for nineteenth-century radicalism. He prompted millions to think in new ways about the world. Because of his deist writings, only six mourners attended Paine's funeral.

Stamp Act Congress

The nine colonies that met in New York City in 1765 did not threaten independence when they vigorously protested the Stamp Act tax, imposed earlier in the year. Parliament had imposed the tax because it was eager to defray the escalating cost of quartering British troops defending the American colonies against Indian forays. It was England's first direct tax on the colonies, and it was levied on purchases in the colonies of legal and commercial documents, licenses, newspapers, pamphlets, almanacs, playing cards, dice, and liquor permits. Sons of Liberty, a newly formed organization of workers, demonstrated in the streets. Particularly vocal were members who were lawyers, editors, printers, and tavern owners. The Stamp Act Congress asserted the right of colonies to freedom from taxation except "with their own consent, given personally, or by their representatives."

Britain repealed the Stamp Act after a year.

The Stamp Act Congress—1765

The Congress met according to adjournment, and resumed, etc., upon mature deliberation agreed to the following declarations of the rights and grievances of the colonists, in America, which were ordered to be inserted . . . the present and impending misfortunes of the British colonies on this continent, having considered as maturely as time will permit the circumstances of the said colonies, esteem it our indispensable duty to make the following declarations of our humble opinion, respecting the most essential rights and liberties of the colonists, and of the grievances under which they labor, by reason of several late acts of Parliament.

1. That His Majesty's subjects in these colonies owe the same allegiance to the Crown of Great Britain that is owing from his subjects born within the Realm, and all due subordination to that august body, the Parliament of Great Britain.

2. That His Majesty's liege subjects in these colonies are entitled to all the inherent rights and liberties of his natural-born subjects within the Kingdom of Great Britain.

3. That it is inseparably essential to the freedom of a people, and the undoubted right of Englishmen, that no taxes be imposed on them but with their own consent, given personally or by their representatives.

4. That the people of these colonies are not, and, from their local circumstances, cannot be represented in the House of Commons in Great Britain.

5. That the only representatives of the people of these colonies are persons chosen therein by themselves, and that no taxes ever have been or can be constitutionally imposed on them but by their respective legislature.

6. That all supplies to the Crown being free gifts of the people, it is unreasonable and inconsistent with the principles and spirit of the British constitution for the people of Great Britain to grant to His Majesty the property of the colonists.

7. That trial by jury is the inherent and invaluable right of every British subject in these colonies.

8. That the late act of Parliament entitled "An act for granting and applying certain stamp duties, and other duties, in the British colonies and plantations in America, etc.," by imposing taxes on the inhabitants of these colonies, and the said act and several other acts by extending the jurisdiction of the Courts of Admiralty beyond its ancient limits, have a manifest tendency to subvert the rights and liberties of the colonists.

9. That the duties imposed by several late acts of Parliament, from the peculiar circumstances of these colonies, will be extremely burdensome and grievous; and from the scarcity of specie, the payment of them absolutely impracticable.

10. That as the profits of the trade of these colonies ultimately center in Great Britain to pay for the manufactures which they are obliged to take from thence, they eventually contribute very largely to all supplies granted there to the Crown.

11. That the restrictions imposed by several late acts of Parliament on the trade of these colonies will render them unable to purchase the manufactures of Great Britain.

12. That the increase, prosperity, and happiness of these colonies depend on the full and free enjoyment of their rights and liberties, and an intercourse with Great Britain mutually affectionate and advantageous.

13. That it is the right of the British subjects in these colonies to petition the King or either house of Parliament.

Lastly. That it is the indispensable duty of these colonies, to the best of sovereigns, to the mother country, and to themselves, to endeavor by a loyal and dutiful address to His Majesty and humble applications to both houses of Parliament, to procure the repeal of the act for granting and applying certain stamp duties, of all clauses of any other acts of Parliament whereby the jurisdiction of the Admiralty is extended as aforesaid, and of the other late acts for the restriction of American commerce.

Olive Branch Petition

In July 1775, American colonists hoped to settle—amicably—differences with the Mother Country over taxation without representation. Negotiations were in the home stretch. War already had erupted in Massachusetts—Lexington, Concord, and then Boston's Bunker Hill (Breed's Hill) were in the history books. Congress's "humble petition," drafted by the Second Continental Congress, was signed by many luminaries, including Thomas Jefferson, Benjamin Franklin, Samuel Adams, John Hancock, Roger Sherman, and Patrick Henry.

A majority of Congressional delegates was ready to declare independence, even if it meant all-out war with the British. A minority felt loyalty to the British Crown, the crown of authority, and favored reconciliation. The majority believed that if King George III did not accept the petition, the minority would join the majority and declare for independence. And so, the delegates agreed to make one more try to have their condition ameliorated and the differences between themselves and Britain settled in a friendly manner. In September 1775, a copy of the humble "Olive Branch" petition was delivered to Lord Dartmouth, Britain's Secretary of State for the Colonies. The petition declared loyalty to the king and the desire for peace.

Congressional representatives in England reported that "his lordship [Dartmouth] promised to deliver [the petition] to his Majesty. We thought it our duty to press his Lordship to obtain an answer; but we were told that his Majesty did not receive it on the throne, no answer would be given." In the next month, George rejected the petition formally, declaring it an illegal document produced by an illegal Congress. He declared the colonies in rebellion.

The Revolutionary War accelerated.

The "Olive Branch" Petitions

To the King's Most Excellent Majesty. Most Gracious Sovereign,

We your Majesty's faithful subjects of the colonies of New-hampshire, Massachusetts-bay, Rhode island and Providence plantations, Connecticut, New-York, New-Jersey, Pennsylvania, the counties of New Castle, Kent and Sussex on Delaware, Maryland, Virginia, North Carolina and South Carolina, in behalf of our-

selves and the inhabitants of these colonies, who have deputed us to represent them in general Congress, entreat your Majesty's gracious attention to this our humble petition.

The union between our Mother Country and these colonies, and the energy of mild and just government, produced benefits so remarkably important, and afforded such an assurance of their permanency and increase, that the wonder and envy of other Nations were excited, while they beheld Great Britain riseing to a power the most extraordinary the world had ever known.

Her rivals observing, that there was no probability of this happy connection being broken by civil dissentions, and apprehending its future effects, if left any longer undisturbed, resolved to prevent her receiving such continual and formidable accessions of wealth and strength, by checking the growth of these settlements from which they were to be derived.

In the prosecution of this attempt events so unfavourable to the design took place, that every friend to the interests of Great Britain and these colonies entertained pleasing and reasonable expectations of seeing an additional force and extention immediately given to the operations of the union hitherto experienced, by an enlargement of the dominions of the Crown, and the removal of ancient and warlike enemies to a greater distance.

At the conclusion therefore of the late war, the most glorious and advantagious that ever had been carried on by British arms, your loyal colonists having con-

tributed to its success, by such repeated and strenuous exertions, as frequently procured them the distinguished approbation of your Majesty, of the late king, and of Parliament, doubted not but that they should be permitted with the rest of the empire, to share in the blessings of peace and the emoluments of victory and conquest. While these recent and honorable acknowledgments of their merits remained on record in the journals and acts of the august legislature the Parliament, undefaced by the imputation or even the suspicion of any offence, they were alarmed by a new system of Statutes and regulations adopted for the administration of the colonies, that filled their minds with the most painful fears and jealousies; and to their inexpressible astonishment perceived the dangers of a foreign quarrel quickly succeeded by domestic dangers, in their judgment of a more dreadful kind.

Nor were their anxieties alleviated by any tendancy in this system to promote the welfare of the Mother Country. For 'tho its effects were more immediately felt by them, yets its influence appeared to be injurious to the commerce and prosperity of Great Britain.

We shall decline the ungrateful task of describing the irksome variety of artifices practised by many of your Majesty's ministers, the delusive pretences, fruitless terrors, and unavailing severities, that have from time to time been dealt out by them, in their attempts to execute this impolitic plan, or of traceing thro' a series of years past the progress of the unhappy differences between Great Britain and these colonies which have flowed from this fatal source.

Your Majestys ministers persevering in their measures and proceeding to open hostilities for enforcing them, have compelled us to arm in our own defence, and have engaged us in a controversy so peculiarly abhorrent to the affection of your still faithful colonists, that when we consider whom we must oppose in this contest, and if it continues, what may be the consequences, our own particular misfortunes are accounted by us, only as parts of our distress.

Knowing, to what violent resentments and incurable animosities, civil discords are apt to exasperate and inflame the contending parties, we think ourselves required by indispensable obligations to Almighty God, to your Majesty, to our fellow subjects, and to ourselves, immediately to use all the means in our power not incompatible with our safety, for stopping the further effusion of blood, and for averting the impending calamities that threaten the British Empire.

Thus called upon to address your Majesty on affairs of such moment to America, and probably to all your dominions, we are earnestly desirous of performing this office with the utmost deference for your Majesty; and we therefore pray, that your royal magnanimity and benevolence may make the most favourable construction of our expressions on so uncommon an occasion. Could we represent in their full force the sentiments that agitate the minds of us your dutiful subjects, we are persuaded, your Majesty would ascribe any seeming deviation from reverence, and our language, and even in our conduct, not to any reprehensible intention but to the impossibility or reconciling the usual appearances of respect with a just attention to our own preservation against those artful and cruel enemies, who abuse your royal confidence and authority for the purpose of effecting our destruction.

Attached to your Majestys person, family and government with all the devotion that principle and affection can inspire, connected with Great Britain by the strongest ties that can unite societies, and deploring every event that tends in any degree to weaken them, we solemnly assure your Majesty, that we not only most ardently desire the former harmony between her and these colonies may be restored but that a concord may be established between them upon so firm a basis, as to perpetuate its blessings uninterrupted by any future dissentions to succeeding generations in both countries, and to transmit your Majestys name to posterity adorned with that signal and lasting glory that has attended the memory of those illustrious personages, whose virtues and abilities have extricated states from dangerous convulsions, and by securing happiness to others, have erected the most noble and durable monuments to their own fame.

We beg leave further to assure your Majesty that notwithstanding the sufferings of your loyal colonists during the course of the present controversy, our breasts retain too tender a regard for the kingdom from which we derive our origin to request such a reconciliation as might in any manner be inconsistent with her dignity or her welfare. These, related as we are to her, honor and duty, as well as inclination induce us to support and advance; and the apprehensions that now oppress our hearts with unspeakable grief, being once removed, your Majesty will find your faithful subjects on this continent ready and willing at all times, as they ever have been with their lives and fortunes to assert and maintain the rights and interests of your Majesty and of our Mother Country.

We therefore beseech your Majesty, that your royal authority and influence may be graciously interposed to procure us releif [sic] from our afflicting fears and jealousies occasioned by the system before mentioned, and to settle peace through every part of your dominions, with all humility submitting to your Majesty's wise consideration, whether it may not be expedient for facilitating those important purposes, that your Majesty be pleased to direct some mode by which the united applications of your faithful colonists to the throne, in pursuance of their common councils, may be improved into a happy and permanent reconciliation; and that in the meantime measures be taken for preventing the further destruction of the lives of your Majesty's subjects; and that such statutes as more immediately distress any of your Majestys colonies be repealed: For by such arrangements as your Majestys wisdom can form for collecting the united sense of your American people, we are convinced, your Majesty would receive such satisfactory proofs of the disposition of the colonists towards their sovereign and the parent state, that the wished for opportunity would soon be restored to them, of evincing the sincerity of their professions by every testimony of devotion becoming the most dutiful subjects and the most affectionate colonists.

That your Majesty may enjoy a long and prosperous reign, and that your descendants may govern your dominions with honor to themselves and happiness to their subjects is our sincere and fervent prayer.

Jefferson

Thomas Jefferson, known for his writing gift, drafted America's birth certificate. He did not want to develop new principles, or new arguments never before thought of. He did not want to say things that never before had been said. The Sage of Monticello wanted to "place before mankind the common sense of the subject," in terms so plain and firm as to command their assent, and "to justify ourself in the independent state we are compelled to take. He was inspired by the harmonizing sentiments of the day. He intended the document simply as "an expression of the American mind." As it turned out, soaring rhetoric suited the Declaration of Independence ideally.

Jefferson's skill in composition and his aptness of expression rose to the occasion. His endlessly roving mind produced another triumph of reason. Nearly a century later, President Abraham Lincoln hailed the Declaration of Independence for throwing off the bonds of tyranny.

On July 2, 1776, delegates of all but one of the colonies had voted in favor of independence. (The thirteenth colony, New York, abstained, awaiting approval from its newly elected convention.) Two days later, the Declaration of

Independence—the great American symbol of independence, revolution, and liberty—was printed.

In 1821, the ambitious Jefferson informed another former president, James Madison, that he had not turned to "book nor pamphlet while writing the Declaration of Independence. I did not consider it as any part of my charge to invent new ideas altogether and to offer no sentiment which had never been expressed before." Later, Jefferson asserted that its authority rested on the harmonizing sentiments of the day, whether expressed in conversation, in letters, printed essays, or the elementary books of public right, as Aristotle, Cicero, Locke, Sidney, etc.

It has been written that the greatness of Jefferson's achievement, aside from the fact that he created one of the outstanding literary documents of the world and of all time, was that he identified its sublime purpose with the roots of liberal traditions that spread back to England, Scotland, Geneva, Holland, Germany, Rome, and Athens. In the fundamental statement of national purpose for a people who were to embrace many races and many creeds, nothing could have been more appropriate than that the act renouncing the ties of consanguinity should draw its philosophical justification from traditions common to all.

Jefferson scored and scratched his rough draft "like a schoolboy's exercises". A fresh draft in Jefferson's hand was delivered to Congress. In Jefferson's view, Congress's "depredations" did a good deal of damage.

Thomas Jefferson's Rough Draught of the Declaration of Independence

A Declaration of the Representatives of the UNITED STATES OF AMERICA, in General Congress assembled.

When in the course of human events it becomes necessary for a people to advance from that subordination in which they have hitherto remained, & to assume among the powers of the earth the equal & independant station to which the laws of nature & of nature's god entitle them, a decent respect to the opinions of mankind requires that they should declare the causes which impel them to the change.

We hold these truths to be sacred & undeniable; that all men are created equal & independant, that from that equal creation they derive rights inherent & inalienable, among which are the preservation of life, & liberty, & the pursuit of happiness; that to secure these ends, governments are instituted among men, deriving their just powers from the consent of the governed; that whenever any form of government shall become destructive of these ends, it is the right of the people to alter or to abolish it, & to institute new government, laying it's foundation on such principles & organising it's powers in such form, as to them shall seem most likely to effect their safety & happiness. prudence indeed will dictate that governments long established should not be changed for light & transient causes: and accordingly all experience hath shewn that mankind are more disposed to suffer while evils are sufferable, than to right themselves by abolishing the forms to which they are accustomed, but when a long train of abuses & usurpations, begun at a distinguished period, & pursuing invariably the same object, evinces a design to subject them to arbitrary power, it is their right, it is their duty, to throw off such government & to provide new guards for their future security, such has been the patient sufferance of these colonies; & such is now the necessity which constrains them to expunge their former systems of government, the history of his present majesty, is a history of unremitting injuries and usurpations, among which no one fact stands single or solitary to contradict the uniform tenor of the rest, all of which have in direct object the establishment of an absolute tyranny over these states, to prove this, let facts be submitted to a candid world, for the truth of which we pledge a faith yet unsullied by falsehood.

he has refused his assent to laws the most wholesome and necessary for the public good:

he has forbidden his governors to pass laws of immediate & pressing importance, unless suspended in their operation till his assent should be obtained; and when so suspended, he has neglected utterly to attend to them.

he has refused to pass other laws for the accomodation of large districts of people unless those people would relinquish the right of representation, a right inestimable to them, & formidable to tyrants alone:

he has dissolved Representative houses repeatedly & continually, for opposing with manly firmness his invasions on the rights of the people:

he has refused for a long space of time to cause others to be elected, whereby the legislative powers, incapable of annihilation, have returned to the people at large for their exercise, the state remaining in the mean time exposed to all the dangers of invasion from without, & convulsions within:

he has endeavored to prevent the population of these states; for that purpose obstructing the laws for naturalization of foreigners; refusing to pass others to encourage their migrations hither; & raising the conditions of new appropriations of lands:

he has suffered the administration of justice totally to cease in some of these colonies, refusing his assent to laws for establishing judiciary powers:

he has made our judges dependant on his will alone, for the tenure of their offices, and amount of their salaries:

he has erected a multitude of new offices by a self-assumed power, & sent hither swarms of officers to harrass our people & eat out their substance:

he has kept among us in times of peace standing armies & ships of war:

he has affected to render the military, independent of & superior to the civil power:

he has combined with others to subject us to a jurisdiction foreign to our constitutions and unacknoleged by our laws; giving his assent to their pretended acts of legislation, for quartering large bodies of armed troops among us;

for protecting them by a mock-trial from punishment for any murders they should commit on the inhabitants of these states;

for cutting off our trade with all parts of the world;

for imposing taxes on us without our consent;

for depriving us of the benefits of trial by jury;

for transporting us beyond seas to be tried for pretended offences:

for taking away our charters, & altering fundamentally the forms of our governments;

for suspending our own legislatures & declaring themselves invested with power to legislate for us in all cases whatsoever:

he has abdicated government here, withdrawing his governors, & declaring us out of his allegiance & protection:

he has plundered our seas, ravaged our coasts, burnt our towns & destroyed the lives of our people:

he is at this time transporting large armies of foreign mercenaries to compleat the works of death, desolation & tyranny, already begun with circumstances of cruelty & perfidy unworthy the head of a civilized nation:

he has endeavored to bring on the inhabitants of our frontiers the merciless Indian savages, whose known rule of warfare is an undistinguished destruction of all ages, sexes, & conditions of existence:

he has incited treasonable insurrections in our fellow-subjects,[10] with the allurements of forfeiture & confiscation of our property:

he has waged cruel war against human nature itself, violating it's most sacred rights of life & liberty in the persons of a distant people who never offended him, captivating & carrying them into slavery in another hemisphere, or to incur miserable death in their transportation thither. this piratical warfare, the opprobrium of infidel powers, is the warfare of the CHRISTIAN king of Great Britain. determined to keep open a market where MEN should be bought & sold, he has prostituted

A Declaration by the Representatives of the UNITED STATES
OF AMERICA, in General Congress assembled.

When in the course of human events it becomes necessary for ~~to~~ one people to
dissolve the political bands which have connected them with another, and to ~~assume~~
~~[among the powers of the earth the]~~ separate and equal station to
which the laws of nature & of nature's god entitle them, a decent respect
to the opinions of mankind requires that they should declare the causes
which impel them to the ~~change~~ separation.

We hold these truths to be ~~sacred & undeniable~~ self-evident; that all men ~~are~~
created equal, ~~& independent;~~ that ~~from that equal creation they derive~~ they are endowed by their creator with
~~rights~~ ~~inherent &~~ inalienable, rights that among these are
life & liberty, & the pursuit of happiness; that to secure these rights, go-
-vernments are instituted among men, deriving their just powers from
the consent of the governed; that whenever any form of government
~~shall~~ becomes destructive of these ends, it is the right of the people to alter
or to abolish it, & to institute new government, laying it's foundation on
such principles & organising it's powers in such form, as to them shall
seem most likely to effect their safety & happiness. prudence indeed
will dictate that governments long established should not be changed for
light & transient causes: and accordingly all experience hath shewn that
mankind are more disposed to suffer while evils are sufferable, than to
right themselves by abolishing the forms to which they are accustomed but
when a long train of abuses & usurpations, [begun at a distinguished period
&] pursuing invariably the same object, evinces a design to ~~subject~~ reduce
them under absolute despotism, it is their right, it is their duty, to throw off such
government & to provide new guards for their future security. such has
been the patient sufferance of these colonies & such is now the necessity
which constrains them to [expunge] their former systems of government.
the history of the present king of Great Britain is a history of [unremitting] injuries and
usurpations. [among which appears no solitary fact but all have] to contra-
-dict the uniform tenor of the rest. [all of which] [have] in direct object the
establishment of an absolute tyranny over these states. to prove this, let facts be
submitted to a candid world, [for the truth of which we pledge a faith
yet unsullied by falsehood.]

he has refused his assent to laws the most wholesome and necessary for the pub.
-lic good.
he has forbidden his governors to pass laws of immediate & pressing importance,
unless suspended in their operation till his assent should be obtained;
and when so suspended, he has utterly neglected attend to attend to them
he has refused to pass other laws for the accomodation of large districts of people
unless those people would relinquish the right of representation in the legislature, a right
inestimable to them & formidable to tyrants only.
he has called together legislative bodies at places unusual, uncomfortable & distant from
the depository of their public records, for the sole purpose of fatiguing them into compliance
with his measures.
he has dissolved Representative houses repeatedly & continually for opposing with
manly firmness his invasions on the rights of the people.
he has refused for a long time after such dissolutions to cause others to be elected.

his negative for suppressing every legislative attempt to prohibit or to restrain this execrable commerce: and that this assemblage of horrors might want no fact of distinguished die, he is now exciting those very people to rise in arms among us, and to purchase that liberty of which he has deprived them, by murdering the people upon whom he also obtruded them; thus paying off former crimes committed against the liberties of one people, with crimes which he urges them to commit against the lives of another.

in every stage of these oppressions we have petitioned for redress in the most humble terms; our repeated petitions have been answered by repeated injury. a prince whose character is thus marked by every act which may define a tyrant, is unfit to be the ruler of a people who mean to be free. future ages will scarce believe that the hardiness of one man, adventured within the short compass of 12 years only, on so many acts of tyranny without a mask, over a people fostered & fixed in principles of liberty.

Nor have we been wanting in attentions to our British brethren. we have warned them from time to time of attempts by their legislature to extend a jurisdiction over these our states. we have reminded them of the circumstances of our emigration & settlement here, no one of which could warrant so strange a pretension: that these were effected at the expence of our own blood & treasure, unassisted by the wealth or the strength of Great Britain: that in constituting indeed our several forms of government, we had adopted one common king, thereby laying a foundation for perpetual league & amity with them: but that submission to their parliament was no part of our constitution, nor ever in idea, if history may be credited: and we appealed to their native justice & magnanimity, as well as to the ties of our common kindred to disavow these usurpations which were likely to interrupt our correspondence & connection. they too have been deaf to the voice of justice & of consanguinity, & when occasions have been given them, by the regular course of their laws, of removing from their councils the disturbers of our harmony, they have by their free election re-established them in power, at this very time too they are permitting their chief magistrate to send over not only soldiers of our common blood, but Scotch & foreign mercenaries to invade & deluge us in blood. these facts have given the last stab to agonizing affection, and manly spirit bids us to renounce for ever these unfeeling brethren. we must endeavor to forget our former love for them, and to hold them as we hold the rest of mankind, enemies in war, in peace friends. we might have been a free & a great people together; but a communication of grandeur & of freedom it seems is below their dignity. be it so, since they will have it: the road to glory & happiness is open to us too; we will climb it in a separate state, and acquiesce in the necessity which pronounces our everlasting Adieu!

We therefore the representatives of the United States of America in General Congress assembled do, in the name & by authority of the good people of these states, reject and renounce all allegiance & subjection to the kings of Great Britain & all others who may hereafter claim by, through, or under them; we utterly dissolve & break off all political connection which may have heretofore subsisted between us & the people or parliament of Great Britain; and finally we do assert and declare these colonies to be free and independant states, and that as free & independant states they shall hereafter have power to levy war, conclude peace, contract alliances, establish commerce, & to do all other acts and things which independant states may of right do. And for the support of this declaration we mutually pledge to each other our lives, our fortunes, & our sacred honour.

A Declaration by the Representatives of the UNITED STATES OF AMERICA in General Congress assembled.

When in the course of human events it becomes necessary for one people to dissolve the political bands which have connected them with another, and to assume among the powers of the earth the separate and equal station to which the laws of nature and of nature's god entitle them, a decent respect to the opinions of mankind requires that they should declare the causes which impel them to the separation.

We hold these truths to be self-evident; that all men are created equal; that they are endowed by their Creator with ~~inherent and~~ certain inalienable rights; that among these are life, liberty, and the pursuit of happiness; that to secure these rights, governments are instituted among men, deriving their just powers from the consent of the governed; that whenever any form of government becomes destructive of these ends, it is the right of the people to alter or to abolish it, and to institute new government, laying it's foundation on such principles, and organising it's powers in such form as to them shall seem most likely to effect their safety and happiness. prudence indeed will dictate that governments long established should not be changed for light & transient causes. and accordingly all experience hath shewn that mankind are more disposed to suffer, while evils are sufferable, than to right themselves by abolishing the forms to which they are accustomed but when a long train of abuses and usurpations, ~~begun at a distinguished period &~~ pursuing invariably the same object, evinces a design to reduce them under absolute despotism, it is their right, it is their duty, to throw off such government & to provide new guards for their future security. such has been the patient sufferance of these colonies; & such is now the necessity which constrains them to ~~expunge~~ _{alter} their former systems of government. the history of the present king of Great Britain, is a history of ~~unremitting~~ _{repeated} injuries and usurpations, ~~among which appears no solitary fact to contradict the uniform tenor of the rest; but~~ all _{having} in direct object the establishment of an absolute tyranny over these states. to prove this let facts be submitted to a candid world, ~~for the truth of which we pledge a faith yet unsullied by falsehood~~.

He has refused his assent to laws the most wholesome and necessary for the public good.

he has forbidden his governors to pass laws of immediate & pressing importance, unless suspended in their operation till his assent should be obtained; and when so suspended, he has _{utterly} neglected ~~utterly~~ to attend to them.

he has refused to pass other laws for the accomodation of large districts of people, unless those people would relinquish the right of representation in the legislature; a right inestimable to them, & formidable to tyrants only.

he has called together legislative bodies at places unusual, uncomfortable, & distant from the depository of their public records, for the sole purpose of fatiguing them into compliance with his measures.

he has dissolved Representative houses repeatedly ~~& continually,~~ for opposing with manly firmness his invasions on the rights of the people.

he has refused for a long time after such dissolutions to cause others to be elected whereby the legislative powers, incapable of annihilation, have returned to the people at large for their exercise, the state remaining in the meantime exposed to all the dangers of invasion from without, & convulsions within.

he has endeavored to prevent the population of these states; for that purpose obstructing the laws for naturalization of foreigners; refusing to pass others to encourage their migrations hither; & raising the conditions of new appropriations of lands.

he has ~~suffered~~ ^{obstructed} the administration of justice ~~totally to cease in some of these states,~~ ^{by} refusing his assent to laws for establishing judiciary powers.

he has made ~~our~~ judges dependent on his will alone, for the tenure of their offices, and the amount & paiment of their salaries.

he has erected a multitude of new offices ~~by a self assumed power,~~ & sent hither swarms of officers to harrass our people, and eat out their substance.

he has kept among us, in time of peace, standing armies ~~and ships of war,~~ with out the consent of our legislatures.

he has affected to render the military independant of, & superior to, the civil power.

he has combined with others to subject us to a jurisdiction foreign to our constitutions and unacknoleged by our laws; giving his assent to their acts of pretended legislation

for quartering large bodies of armed troops among us;

for protecting them by a mock-trial from punishment for any murders which they should commit on the inhabitants of these states;

for cutting off our trade with all parts of the world;

for imposing taxes on us without our consent;

for depriving us ^{in many cases} of the benefits of trial by jury;

for transporting us beyond seas to be tried for pretended offences;

for abolishing the free system of English laws in a neighboring province, establishing therein an arbitrary government and enlarging it's boundaries so as to render it at once an example & fit instrument for introducing the same absolute rule into these states.[2]

for taking away our charters abolishing our most valuable laws, and altering fundamentally the forms of our governments;

for suspending our own legislatures, & declaring themselves invested with power to legislate for us in all cases whatsoever.

he has abdicated government here , ~~withdrawing his governors, &~~ by declaring us out of his ~~allegiance and~~ protection, and waging war against us.

he has plundered our seas, ravaged our coasts, burnt our towns, & destroyed the lives of our people.

he is at this time transporting large armies of foreign mercenaries, to compleat the works of death, desolation & tyranny, already begun with circumstances of cruelty & perfidy, scarcely paralleled in the most barbarous ages and totally unworthy the head of a civilized nation.

he has endeavored to bring on the inhabitants of our frontiers the merciless excited domestic insurrections amongst us and has Indian savages, whose known rule of warfare is an undistinguished destruction of all ages, sexes & conditions ~~of existence.~~

~~he has incited treasonable insurrections of our fellow citizens, with the allurements of forfeiture & confiscation of property.~~

he has constrained , our fellow citizens ~~others;~~[3] taken captives on the high seas to bear arms against their country, to become the executioners of their friends & brethren, or to fall themselves by their hands.

~~he has waged cruel war against human nature itself, violating it's most sacred~~
~~rights of life & liberty in the persons of a distant people, who never offended him,~~
~~captivating and carrying them into slavery in another hemisphere, or to incur miser-~~
~~able death in their transportation thither. this piratical warfare, the opprobrium of~~
~~infidel powers, is the warfare of the Christian king of Great Britain. determined to~~
~~keep open a market where MEN should be bought & sold, he has prostituted his~~
~~negative for suppressing every legislative attempt to prohibit or to restrain this exe-~~
~~crable commerce: and that this assemblage of horrors might want no fact of distin-~~
~~guished die, he now is now exciting these very people to rise in arms among us, and~~
~~to purchase that liberty of which he has deprived them, by murdering the people upon~~
~~whom he also obtruded them: thus paying off former crimes committed against the~~
~~liberties of one people, with crimes which he urges them to commit against the lives~~
~~of another.~~

In every stage of these oppressions, we have petitioned for redress in the most
humble terms; our repeated petitions have been answered only by repeated injury a
prince whose character is thus marked by every act which may define a tyrant, is
unfit to be the ruler of a _{free} ~~people who mean to be free future ages will scarce believe~~
~~that the hardiness of one man adventured within the short compass of twelve years~~
~~only; to build a foundation, so broad and undisguised, for tyranny over a people fos-~~
~~tered and fixed in principles of freedom.~~

Nor have we been wanting in attentions to our British brethren. we have warned
them from time to time of attempts by their legislature to extend ~~a~~ ^{an unwarrantable} jurisdiction
over ^{us} ~~these our states~~ we have reminded them of the circumstances of our emigration and settlement here, ~~no one of which could warrant so strange a pretension;~~
~~that these were effected at the expence of our own blood and treasure, unassisted by~~
~~the wealth or the strength of Great Britain: that in constituting indeed our several~~

~~forms of government, we had adopted one common king; thereby laying a foundation~~

~~for perpetual league and amity with them: but that submission to their parliament~~

have

~~was no part of our constitution, or ever in idea, if history may be credited:~~ and we

and we have conjured them by

appealed to their native justice & magnanimity, ~~as well as to~~ the tyes of our com-

would inevitably

mon kindred, to disavow these usurpations, which ~~were likely to~~ interrupt our con-

nections & correspondence they too have been deaf to the voice of justice and of

consanguinity; ~~and when occasions have been given them, by the regular course of~~

~~their laws, of removing from their councils the disturbers of our harmony, they have~~

~~by their free election re-established them in power at this very time too, they are per-~~

~~mitting their chief magistrate to send over not only soldiers of our common blood,~~

~~but Scotch and foreign mercenaries to invade and destroy us these facts have given~~

~~the last stab to agonizing affection; and manly spirit bids us to renounce forever~~

therefore

~~these unfeeling brethren:~~ we must ~~endeavor to forget our former love for them, and to~~

~~hold them, as we hold the rest of mankind, enemies in war, in peace friends we~~

~~might have been a free & a great people together; but a communication of grandeur~~

~~and of freedom, it seems, is below their dignity be it so, since they will have it the~~

~~road to happiness and to glory is open to us too; we will climb it apart from them~~

is & ought to be totally dissolved;

~~and~~ acquiesce in the necessity which denounces our ~~eternal~~ separation and hold

them, as we hold the rest of mankind, enemies in war, in peace friends.

We therefore the Representatives of the United states of America, in General

appealing to the supreme judge of the world for the rectitude of our intentions,

Congress assembled, do, in the name and by authority of the good people of these

colonies, solemnly publish and declare, that these united colonies are and of right ought to be

~~states, reject~~ free and independent states; that they are absolved from all allegiance

to the British Crown, and that ~~and renounce all allegiance and subjection to the~~

~~kings of Great Britain, & all others who may hereafter claim by, through, or under~~

~~them; we utterly dissolve~~ all political connection ~~which may heretofore have sub-~~

them   state   is thought to be totally dissolved;

~~sisted~~ between ~~us~~ and the ~~parliament or people~~ of Great Britain ~~and finally we do~~

40

as~~sert~~ ~~[and~~ ~~declare]~~[+] these colonies to be free and independant states, ~~& that as free~~ ~~& independent states, they have full power to levy war, conclude peace, contract~~ ~~alliances, establish commerce, & to do all other acts and things which independant~~ with a firm reliance on the protection of divine providence, ~~states may of right do. And for the support of this declaration,~~ ∧we mutually pledge to each other our lives, our fortunes, and our sacred honor.

The Declaration of Final Version
Independence 1776

When in the Course of human events, it becomes necessary for one people to dissolve the political bands which have connected them with another, and to assume among the Powers of the earth, the separate and equal station to which the Laws of Nature and of Nature's God entitle them, a decent respect to the opinions of mankind requires that they should declare the causes which impel them to the separation.

  We hold these truths to be self-evident, that all men are created equal, that they

are endowed by their Creator with certain unalienable Rights, that among these are Life, Liberty and the pursuit of Happiness. That to secure these rights, Governments are instituted among Men, deriving their just powers from the consent of the governed. That whenever any Form of Government becomes destructive of these ends, it is the Right of the People to alter or to abolish it, and to institute new Government, laying its foundation on such principles and organizing its powers in such form, as to them that shall seem most likely to effect their Safety and Happiness. Prudence, indeed, will dictate that Governments long established should not be changed for light and transient causes; and accordingly all experience hath shown, that mankind are more disposed to suffer, while evils are sufferable, than to right themselves by abolishing the forms to which they are accustomed. But when a long train of abuses and usurpations, pursuing invariably the same Object evinces a design to reduce them under absolute Despotism, it is their right, it is their duty, to throw off such Government, and to provide new Guards for their future security.—Such has been the patient sufferance of these Colonies; and such is now the necessity which constrains them to alter their former Systems of Government. The history of the present King of Great Britain is a history of repeated injuries and usurpations, all having in direct object the establishment of an absolute Tyranny over these States. To prove this, let Facts be submitted to a candid world.

He has refused his Assent to Laws, the most wholesome and necessary for the public good.

He has forbidden his Governors to pass Laws of immediate and pressing importance, unless suspended in their operation till his Assent should be obtained; and when so suspended, he has utterly neglected to attend to them.

He has refused to pass other Laws for the accommodation of large districts of people, unless those people would relinquish the right of Representation in the Legislature, a right inestimable to them and formidable to tyrants only.

He has called together legislative bodies at places unusual, uncomfortable, and distant from the depository of their Public Records, for the sole purpose of fatiguing them into compliance with his measures.

He has dissolved Representative Houses repeatedly, for opposing with manly firmness his invasions on the rights of the people.

He has refused for a long time, after such dissolutions, to cause others to be elected; whereby the Legislative Powers, incapable of Annihilation, have returned to the People at large for their exercise; the State remaining in the mean time exposed to all the dangers of invasion from without, and convulsions within.

He has endeavoured to prevent the population of these States; for that purpose obstructing the Laws of Naturalization of Foreigners; refusing to pass others to encourage their migration hither, and raising the conditions of new Appropriations of Lands.

He has obstructed the Administration of Justice, by refusing his Assent to Laws for establishing Judiciary Powers.

He has made Judges dependent on his Will alone, for the tenure of their offices, and the amount and payment of their salaries.

He has erected a multitude of New Offices, and sent hither swarms of Offices to harass our People, and eat out their substance.

He has kept among us, in times of peace, Standing Armies without the Consent of our legislature.

He has affected to render the Military independent of and superior to the Civil Power.

He has combined with others to subject us to a jurisdiction foreign to our constitution, and unacknowledged by our laws; giving his Assent to their acts of pretended legislation:

For quartering large bodies of armed troops among us:

For protecting them, by a mock Trial, from Punishment for any Murders which they should commit on the Inhabitants of these States:

For cutting off our Trade with all parts of the world:

For imposing taxes on us without our Consent:

For depriving us in many cases, of the benefits of Trial by Jury:

For transporting us beyond Seas to be tried for pretended offences:

For abolishing the free System of English Laws in a neighboring Province, establishing therein an Arbitrary government, and enlarging its Boundaries so as to render it at once an example and fit instrument for introducing the same absolute rule into these Colonies:

For taking away our Charters, abolishing our most valuable Laws, and altering fundamentally the Forms of our Governments:

For suspending our own Legislature, and declaring themselves invested with Power to legislate for us in all cases whatsoever.

He has abdicated Government here, by declaring us out of his Protection and waging War against us.

He has plundered our seas, ravaged our Coasts, burnt our towns, and destroyed the lives of our people.

He is at this time transporting large armies of foreign mercenaries to compleat the works of death, desolation and tyranny, already begun with circumstances of

Cruelty & perfidy scarcely paralleled in the most barbarous ages, and totally unworthy the Head of a civilized nation.

He has constrained our fellow Citizens taken Captive on the high Seas to bear Arms against their Country, to become the executioners of their friends and Brethren, or to fall themselves by their Hands.

He has excited domestic insurrections amongst us, and has endeavoured to bring on the inhabitants of our frontiers, the merciless Indian Savages, whose known rule of warfare, is an undistinguished destruction of all ages, sexes and conditions.

In every stage of these Oppressions We have Petitioned for Redress in the most humble terms: Our repeated Petitions have been answered only by repeated injury. A Prince, whose character is thus marked by every act which may define a Tyrant, is unfit to be the ruler of a free People.

Nor have We been wanting in attention to our British brethren. We have warned them from time to time of attempts by their legislature to extend an unwarrantable jurisdiction over us. We have reminded them of the circumstances of our emigration and settlement here. We have appealed to their native justice and magnanimity, and we have conjured them by the ties of our common kindred to disavow these usurpations, which, would inevitably interrupt our connections and correspondence. They too have been deaf to the voice of justice and of consanguinity. We must, therefore, acquiesce in the necessity, which denounces our Separation, and hold them, as we hold the rest of mankind, Enemies in War, in Peace Friends.

We, therefore, the Representatives of the United States of America, in General Congress, Assembled, appealing to the Supreme Judge of the world for the rectitude of our intentions, do, in the Name, and by Authority of the good People of these Colonies, solemnly publish and declare, That these United Colonies are, and of Right ought to be Free and Independent States; that they are Absolved from all Allegiance to the British Crown, and that all political connection between them and the State of Great Britain, is and ought to be totally dissolved; and that as Free and Independent States, they have full Power to levy War, conclude Peace, contract Alliances, establish Commerce, and to do all other Acts and Things which Independent States may of right do. And for the support of this Declaration, with a firm reliance on the Protection of Divine Providence, we mutually pledge to each other our Lives, our Fortunes and our sacred Honor.

JOHN HANCOCK

New Hampshire
JOSIAH BARTLETT
WM. WHIPPLE
MATTHEW THORNTON

Massachusetts-Bay
SAML. ADAMS
JOHN ADAMS
ROBT. TREAT PAINE
ELBRIDGE GERRY

Rhode Island
STEP. HOPKINS
WILLIAM ELLERY

Connecticut
ROGER SHERMAN
SAM'EL HUNTINGTON
WM. WILLIAMS
OLIVER WOLCOTT

New York
WM. FLOYD
PHIL. LIVINGSTON
FRANS. LEWIS
LEWIS MORRIS

Pennsylvania
ROBT. MORRIS
BENJAMIN RUSH
BENJA. FRANKLIN
JOHN MORTON
GEO. CLYMER
JAS. SMITH
GEO. TAYLOR
JAMES WILSON
GEO. ROSS

Delaware
CAESAR RODNEY
GEO. READ
THO. M'KEAN

North Carolina
WM. HOOPER
JOSEPH HEWES
JOHN PENN

South Carolina
EDWARD RUTLEDGE
THOS. HEYWARD, JUNR.
THOMAS LYNCH, JUNR.
ARTHUR MIDDLETON

New Jersey
RICHD. STOCKTON
JNO. WITHERSPOON
FRAS. HOPKINSON
JOHN HART
ABRA. CLARK

Georgia
BUTTON GWINNETT
LYMAN HALL
GEO. WALTON

Maryland
SAMUEL CHASE
WM. PACA
THOS. STONE
CHARLES CARROLL
OF CARROLLTON

Virginia
GEORGE WYTHE
RICHARD HENRY LEE
TH. JEFFERSON
BENJA. HARRISON
THS. NELSON, JR.
FRANCIS LIGHTFOOT LEE
CARTER BRAXTON

The Second of July: Hurrah!!!!

John Adams, the pragmatic Boston rebel and political theorist, recounted what happened when Congress appointed a committee of five to write a declaration of independence:

"The committee appointed Mr. Jefferson and me, to draw them (i.e., the Articles) up in form, and cloath them in a proper dress. The Sub Committee . . . considered the Minutes, making such Observations on them as then occurred: when Mr. Jefferson desired me to take them to my Lodgings and make the Draught. This I declined and gave several reasons for declining. 1. That he was a Virginian and I a Massachusettensian. 2. That he was a southern Man and I a Northern one. 3. That I had been so obnoxious for my early and constant Zeal in promoting the Measure, that any draught of mine would undergo a more severe Scrutiny and Criticism in Congress, than one of his composition. 4thly and lastly, that would be reason enough if there were no other, I had a great Opinion of the Elegance of his pen and none at all of my own . . . He accordingly took the Minutes and in a day or two produced to me his Draught. . . ."

John Adams, a fearless advocate of independence, told his wife, Abigail, that "America was getting a whole government of our own choice, managed by persons

IN CONGRESS. JULY 4. 1776.

The unanimous Declaration of the thirteen united States of America,

He has abdicated Government here, by declaring us out of his Protection and waging War against us. — He has plundered our seas, ravaged our Coasts, burnt our Towns, and destroyed the Lives of our people. — He is at this time transporting large Armies of foreign Mercenaries to compleat the works of death, desolation and tyranny, already begun with circumstances of Cruelty & perfidy scarcely paralleled in the most barbarous ages, and totally unworthy the Head of a civilized nation. — He has constrained our fellow Citizens taken Captive on the high Seas to bear Arms against their Country, to become the executioners of their friends and Brethren, or to fall themselves by their Hands. — He has excited domestic insurrections amongst us, and has endeavoured to bring on the inhabitants of our frontiers, the merciless Indian Savages, whose known rule of warfare, is an undistinguished destruction of all ages, sexes and conditions. — In every stage of these Oppressions We have Petitioned for Redress in the most humble terms: Our repeated Petitions have been answered only by repeated injury. A Prince whose character is thus marked by every act which may define a Tyrant, is unfit to be the ruler of a free people. — Nor have We been wanting in attentions to our Brittish brethren. We have warned them from time to time of attempts by their legislature to extend an unwarrantable jurisdiction over us. We have reminded them of the circumstances of our emigration and settlement here. We have appealed to their native justice and magnanimity, and we have conjured them by the ties of our common kindred to disavow these usurpations, which, would inevitably interrupt our connections and correspondence. They too have been deaf to the voice of justice and of consanguinity. We must, therefore, acquiesce in the necessity, which denounces our Separation, and hold them, as we hold the rest of mankind, Enemies in War, in Peace Friends.

We, therefore, the Representatives of the united States of America, in General Congress, Assembled, appealing to the Supreme Judge of the world for the rectitude of our intentions, do, in the Name, and by Authority of the good People of these Colonies, solemnly publish and declare, That these United Colonies are, and of Right ought to be Free and Independent States; that they are Absolved from all Allegiance to the British Crown, and that all political connection between them and the State of Great Britain, is and ought to be totally dissolved; and that as Free and Independent States, they have full Power to levy War, conclude Peace, contract Alliances, establish Commerce, and to do all other Acts and Things which Independent States may of right do. — And for the support of this Declaration, with a firm reliance on the Protection of divine Providence, we mutually pledge to each other our Lives, our Fortunes and our sacred Honor.

John Hancock

Button Gwinnett
Lyman Hall
Geo Walton.

Wm Hooper
Joseph Hewes,
John Penn

Edward Rutledge.
Thos Heyward Junr.
Thomas Lynch Junr.
Arthur Middleton

Samuel Chase
Wm Paca
Thos Stone
Charles Carroll of Carrollton

George Wythe
Richard Henry Lee
Th Jefferson
Benja Harrison
Thos Nelson jr.
Francis Lightfoot Lee
Carter Braxton

Robt Morris
Benjamin Rush
Benja Franklin
John Morton
Geo Clymer
Jas Smith
Geo Taylor
James Wilson
Geo Ross

Caesar Rodney
Geo Read
Tho McKean

Wm Floyd
Phil Livingston
Frans Lewis
Lewis Morris

Richd Stockton
Jno Witherspoon
Fras Hopkinson
John Hart
Abra Clark

Josiah Bartlett
Wm Whipple
Saml Adams
John Adams
Robt Treat Paine
Elbridge Gerry
Step Hopkins
William Ellery
Roger Sherman
Saml Huntington
Wm Williams
Oliver Wolcott
Matthew Thornton

whom we love, revere, and can confide in, has charms in it, for which men will fight."

Congress issued a legal act of political independence when it adopted the Lee Resolution of Independence on July 2. This prompted Adams, knowing there'd be no turning back, to inform his wife that "The second day of July 1776, will be the most memorable epoch in the history of America. I am apt to believe that it will be celebrated by succeeding generations as the great anniversary Festival. It ought to be commemorated, as the day of deliverance, by solemn acts of devotion to God almighty. It ought to be solemnized with pomp and parade, with shows, games, sports, guns, bells, bonfires, and illuminations, from one end of this continent to the other, from this time forward, forevermore." The Sage of Quincy, always insisted that passage of the Declaration of Independence was merely an ornamental occasion bereft of any larger historical significance. There was no right date to celebrate adoption. Adams actually believed that the decisive moment had occurred on May 15, 1776, the day that the Continental Congress had passed a resolution calling for new constitutions in each of the states, creating separate and independent American governments. The signators if caught by the British, could have been executed for treason.

"The Votaries of Independence"

John Adams

JOHN ADAMS (Massachusetts; 1735-1826)
"Atlas of American Independence" ▪ Second U.S. President ▪ First Vice President ▪ Truculent, erudite ▪ Lawyer, defended British soldiers in Boston Massacre ▪ Proposes George Washington for General of the Army ▪ Vigorously argues for separation ▪ Son John Quincy sixth U.S. President

Sam'l Adams

SAMUEL ADAMS (Massachusetts; 1722–1803)
Radical, second cousin of John Adams ▪ Opposed royal governors ▪ Graduate, Harvard (1740) ▪ Master polemicist ▪ Boston tax collector (1756–1764) ▪ Inept businessman ▪ Instigated Boston Tea Party ▪ Formed Boston's Committee of Correspondence (1773) ▪ Organized Sons of Lib-

erty ▪ Governor, Massachusetts (1794–1797) ▪ Tireless supporter of Declaration of Independence

Josiah Bartlett

JOSIAH BARTLETT (New Hampshire; 1729–1795)
First signatory after the presiding officer, Medical agent, Battle of Bennington ▪ Congressman 1775, 1776, 1778 ▪ Twice Governor, New Hampshire ▪ Chief Justice, N.H. Court of Common Pleas ▪ Declined election to U.S. Senate

Carter Braxton

CARTER BRAXTON (Virginia; 1736–1797)
College of William and Mary ▪ Cambridge University, three years ▪ Filled Congressional vacancy caused by death of delegate ▪ Overcame pro-British stance ▪ Fathered sixteen children

Charles Carroll of Carrollton

CHARLES CARROLL (Maryland; 1737–1832)
Only Catholic among the signers ▪ First U.S. millionaire ▪ Dies at age 95 ▪ Sought Canadian aid during Revolution ▪ Studied civil law in France ▪ Studied common law in London ▪ Resigned U.S. Senate seat to return to Maryland legislature; his political views were conservative ▪ Helped to establish Baltimore and Ohio RR (1828) ▪ Last surviving signatory, dying at age 95

Samuel Chase

SAMUEL CHASE (Maryland; 1741–1811)
"Bacon Face" failed to induce Canada to join revolution against Britain ▪ Supreme Court justice; appointed by President Washington ▪ Acquitted, impeachment charge during Presidency of Thomas Jefferson ▪ Checkered career

ABRAHAM CLARK (New Jersey; 1726–1794)
Cynical, poor man's lawyer, "Man of the people" ▪ Long-time Congressman
▪ Urged Bill of Rights amendments to Constitution

GEORGE CLYMER (PENNSYLVANIA; 1739–1813)
Lifelong friend to George Washington ▪ Active patriot ▪ Captain, volunteer
company, at outbreak of war with Britain ▪ Negotiated treaty with Cherokee and with Creek ▪ Prosperous merchant ▪ Declaration of Independence
his "dearest wish" ▪ Delegate, Constitutional Convention (1787)

WILLIAM ELLERY (Rhode Island; 1727–1820)
Harvard (1747) ▪ Naval officer ▪ Lawyer ▪ Chief Justice, Rhode Island, 30
years ▪ Collector, Port of Newport (1790–1820) ▪ Prolific letter-writer

WILLIAM FLOYD (New York; 1734–1821)
Major General, militia ▪ Congressman (1774–1776; 1779–1783) ▪ Voted with
the "zealous friends of liberty and independence"

BENJAMIN FRANKLIN (Pennsylvania; 1706–1790)
Age: 70 (oldest, most eminent signer), world celebrity ▪ Tenth child of a
chandler ▪ Only two years formal schooling ▪ Polymath, an oracle of wis-

dom • Plan of Union (1754) proposed common-cause scheme for uniting colonies against American Indians, providing mutual defense • Deputy postmaster general for the colonies • Helped to establish first circulating library in America • Founder, American Philosophical Society for the Promotion of Useful Knowledge • U.S. diplomat in France • Minister to Sweden • Represented Pennsylvania in London • Largest funeral in Philadelphia history

Elbridge Gerry

ELBRIDGE GERRY (Massachusetts; 1744–1814)
Third of twelve children • Harvard (1764) • Helped father's shipping business prosper • "Gerrymander" describes redistricting for political advantage • Declines to sign Constitution • Died in debt as U.S. vice president

Button Gwinnett

BUTTON GWINNETT (Georgia; 1735–1777)
Emigrated, England (1765) • Rice planter, St. Catherine's Island • Signature rare, valuable • Died after pistol duel

Lyman Hall

LYMAN HALL (Georgia; 1725–1790)
Yale College (theology, medicine) • Rice planter • Moved north to Connecticut after British despoiled homestead • Returned to Georgia, elected governor (1783) • Helped establish University of Georgia and Franklin College

John Hancock

JOHN HANCOCK (Massachusetts; 1737–1793)
First signatory, boldly declared, "There, I guess King George will be able to read that." • Classics student, Harvard (1754) • Born in relative poverty, son of a parson • Raised from age seven by wealthy uncle • Smuggler • "I

will not be a slave." ▪ Flees Lexington, Massachusetts, to Philadelphia (1775) ▪ Resisted the Stamp Act ▪ Wanted to be Commander of Continental Army ▪ A "patriot in purple" ▪ President, Continental Congress ▪ Mediated differences among the delegations ▪ Nine times governor, Massachusetts ▪ Suffered from gout

Benj. Harrison (signature)

BENJAMIN HARRISON (Virginia; 1726–1791)
Age 50 ▪ Classics student, College of William and Mary ▪ Championed colonialism ▪ Member, House of Burgesses, twenty-five years; sometime House Speaker ▪ Lukewarm to independence ▪ Virginia governor three years ▪ Presided over debates on the Declaration ▪ Son, William Henry Harrison, is eighth U.S. President; great grandson is twenty-fifth President

John Hart (signature)

JOHN HART (New Jersey; 1713–1779)
Owner, grist mill ▪ General Assemblyman, several times ▪ Chairman, New Jersey Council of Safety ▪ Member, Continental Congress, two months (1776) ▪ Fled British forces, hid in mountains ▪ "Honest John"

Joseph Hewes (signature)

JOSEPH HEWES (North Carolina; 1730–1779)
"One of the best and most agreeable men in the world." ▪ Princeton ▪ Bachelor ▪ Abandoned Quakerism at the outbreak of the Revolution. ▪ Profitable mercantiler ▪ Prosperous shipper and merchant ▪ Virtually first head of U.S. Navy ▪ Ardent colonial patriot ▪ At age 48, oldest member of N.C. delegation

Thos. Heyward Junr. (signature)

THOMAS HEYWARD, Jr. (South Carolina; 1746–1809)
Aristocratic planter, lawyer, jurist ▪ Studied law, Middle Temple, London ▪ Imprisoned when British captured Charleston, South Carolina ▪ Signature

on Declaration of Independence said to be least legible ▪ First president, Agricultural Society of South Carolina

ᵞ/ᵐ Hooper

WILLIAM HOOPER (North Carolina; 1742–1790)
Boston's Latin School ▪ Harvard College ▪ Member, landed aristocracy ▪ Lawyer ▪ A "firm republican" ▪ Wrote articles that attacked the Crown ▪ Not present when Declaration of Independence was approved ▪ Commissioner, settled boundary dispute between Massachusetts and New York ▪ Favored adoption of Constitution; a leading orator

Steph. Hopkins

STEPHEN HOPKINS (Rhode Island; 1707–1791)
Second oldest signatory (69) ▪ Good humored ▪ Colonial governor, Rhode Island, nine times ▪ First chancellor, Rhode Island College ▪ Mercantiler

Fra⁸ Hopkinson

FRANCIS HOPKINSON (New Jersey; 1737–1791)
Graduate, College of Philadelphia (now University of Pennsylvania) ▪ Designed first national flag authorized by Congress (1777) ▪ Harpsichordist, caricaturist ▪ First American composer of secular songs ▪ Judge, Admiralty Court, Pennsylvania, several times ▪ Judge, U.S. Court, Eastern District (1789–1791)

Sam ᵘ Huntington

SAMUEL HUNTINGTON (Connecticut; 1731–1796)
Barrelmaker ▪ Lawyer ▪ President, Continental Congress (1779–1781) ▪ Lieutenant Governor, Connecticut (1785) ▪ Governor, Connecticut, twelve years ▪ Parsimonious

Th Jefferson

THOMAS JEFFERSON (Virginia; 1743–July 4, 1826)
Meticulous, graceful mind, slim, red-haired, over six feet tall ▪ Wrote own tombstone: "Here was buried Thomas Jefferson, author of the Declaration of Independence, of the Stature of Virginia for religious freedom; and father of the University of Virginia." ▪ Substitute delegate, Second Continental Congress ▪ Governor, Virginia ▪ U.S. minister, France ▪ First U.S. secretary of state ▪ President, American Philosophical Society ▪ Second U.S. vice president (1797–1801) ▪ Third President (effecting Louisiana Purchase, doubling size of U.S.) ▪ Prophet of progress, symbolized the idea of freedom

Richard Henry Lee

RICHARD HENRY LEE (Virginia; 1732–1794)
Brother, Francis Lightfoot Lee ▪ Educated in Europe ▪ "Cicero" ▪ Offered resolution for independence (June 7, 1776), leading to composition of Declaration of Independence ▪ Aggressive patriot ▪ Closely allied with Thomas Jefferson ▪ Prominent member, House of Burgesses, seventeen years ▪ Opposed Constitution without Bill of Rights ▪ Author, first national Thanksgiving Day proclamation (1777) ▪ Ill health forces resignation from U.S. Senate

Francis Lightfoot Lee

FRANCIS LIGHTFOOT LEE (Virginia; 1734–1797)
Younger brother of Richard Henry Lee ▪ Ardent patriot ▪ Last-minute signatory, replaced another Virginia delegate ▪ Member, Virginia House of Delegates, Virginia Senate ▪ Strongly favored the new Constitution

Fran' Lewis

FRANCIS LEWIS (New York; 1713–1803)
Born, Wales ▪ Attended London schools ▪ Merchant ▪ Contracted to clothe British troops in America (1753) ▪ Prisoner during French-Indian War; on

repatriation, given 500 acres of land by colonial government ▪ Continental Congress (1775–1779) ▪ Commissioner, Board of Admiralty (1779)

Phil. Livingston

PHILIP LIVINGSTON (New York; 1716–1778)
Yale (1737) ▪ Wealthy ▪ Aristocratic philanthropist ▪ Stamp Act Congressman ▪ Helped to establish King's College (today, Columbia University)

Thomas Lynch Junr

THOMAS LYNCH, Jr. (South Carolina; 1749–1779)
Captain, Revolutionary War ▪ Did not seek reelection to Congress ▪ Precarious health after bilious fever ▪ (Ill father had been S.C. delegate) ▪ Lost at sea at age 30

Tho M. Kean

THOMAS MCKEAN (Delaware; 1734–1817)
Vigorous lawyer: Delaware, New Jersey, Pennsylvania ▪ President ▪ Congress, five months ▪ President, Delaware (1777) ▪ Chief Justice ▪ Pennsylvania (1777–1779) ▪ Three-term governor, Pennsylvania, 1799–1808 ▪ Strongly supported Constitution ▪ Last of the signers

Arthur Middleton

ARTHUR MIDDLETON (South Carolina; 1742–1787)
Classics scholar ▪ Cambridge University ▪ Law student, London ▪ Planter, South Carolina ▪ Father owned 800 slaves ▪ Public-spirited capricious aristocrat; mean tempered ▪ British prisoner (May, 1780–July, 1781) ▪ Governor ▪ State senator

LEWIS MORRIS (New York; 1726–1798)
Yale (1746) ▪ Wealthy ▪ Commanded Westchester militia ▪ Member, first Board of Regents, University of New York (1784–1798) ▪ Country gentleman

ROBERT MORRIS (Pennsylvania; 1734–1806)
Emigrated Liverpool, England (1747) ▪ Mercantiler ▪ Superintendent of Finance (1781–1784) ▪ Personal credit prevented U.S. bankruptcy ▪ Secured funds needed to transport troops from New York to Yorktown, Virginia where British surrendered ▪ Declined to be Secretary of Treasury in President Washington's Cabinet ▪ Established Bank of North America ▪ Superintendent of Finance (1781–1784) ▪ Debtors' prison (speculated in western lands) ▪ Died in obscurity

JOHN MORTON (Pennsylvania; 1724–1777)
Swedish stock ▪ Land surveyor ▪ Member, Stamp Act Congress ▪ Associate Justice, Supreme Court of Appeals ▪ Pennsylvania ▪ Persuaded other Pennsylvania delegates to vote for independence: "the most glorious service I ever rendered my country." ▪ First signer to die

THOMAS NELSON, Jr. (Virginia; 1738–1789)
Aristocrat ▪ Cambridge University ▪ Commanded Virginia forces (1777) ▪ Extremely patriotic ▪ Governor ▪ Virginia (1781), succeeding Governor Jefferson

WILLIAM PACA (Maryland; 1740–1799)
Studied law, Annapolis, London ▪ Delegate, first two Continental Congresses ▪ Chief judge, Superior Court, Maryland ▪ Governor, 1782–1785 ▪ Judge, U.S. Court for Maryland (1789–1799)

ROBERT TREAT PAINE (Massachusetts; 1731–1814)

Harvard (1749) ▪ Lawyer ▪ Chaplain on northern frontier, French-Indian War ▪ Signed Olive Branch petition, the final appeal to Crown to settle colonial differences short of war ▪ Prosecutor, murder trial of British soldiers, Boston Massacre ▪ First Massachusetts attorney general ▪ Founder, American Academy of Arts and Sciences ▪ Astronomer

JOHN PENN (North Carolina; 1741–1788)

Very popular ▪ Influenced by Thomas Paine's *Common Sense* ▪ Moved from Virginia ▪ Endorsed Articles of Confederation, duly signed the Declaration of Independence ▪ Diligent lawyer

GEORGE READ (Delaware; 1733–1798)

Head lawyer ▪ Headed Delaware delegation, Constitutional Convention ▪ Encouraged Delaware to ratify Constitution of Delaware (first state to do so) ▪ U.S. Senator ▪ Resigned senatorship to become Chief Justice, Delaware

CAESAR RODNEY (Delaware; 1728–1784)

"His face is not bigger than a large apple" ▪ Farmer ▪ Sheriff ▪ Justice of the peace ▪ Rode horseback from near Dover, Delaware, to Philadelphia to vote for Declaration of Independence ▪ General, Revolutionary Army ▪ President, Delaware (1778–1781) ▪ Speaker, Upper House, State legislature ▪ Elected twice to Congress, does not serve ▪ Dies from cancerous growth on face

Gro. Ross (signature)

GEORGE ROSS (Pennsylvania; 1730–1779)
Scottish stock ▪ Lawyer ▪ Once staunch Loyalist ▪ Judge of the Admiralty
Court of Pennsylvania

Benjamin Rush (signature)

BENJAMIN RUSH (Pennsylvania; 1745–1813)
Vivacious, inpulsive, indiscrete ▪ Medical student, England, Paris ▪ Professor of chemistry, College of Philadelphia ▪ Surgeon general, Revolutionary
War ▪ Quixotic dogmatic ▪ Famous physician, medical teacher ▪ Battled
yellow-fever epidemic, Philadelphia (1793) ▪ Established first free dispensary in U.S. ▪ Sought removal of George Washington as army commander-in-chief ▪ Fathered thirteen children ▪ Founder, Dickinson College ▪
Treasurer, U.S. Mint (1799–1813) ▪ Long-time Federalist, with John Adams
and Thomas Jefferson, brought about renewal of the ex-presidents' correspondence

Edward Rutledge (signature)

EDWARD RUTLEDGE (South Carolina; 1747–1800)
Youngest signatory ▪ Studied law, London ▪ British prisoner, St. Augustine,
Florida ▪ Did not accept President Washington's appointment as Supreme
Court Justice ▪ Staunch Federalist ▪ Governor, South Carolina, died before
completing term

Roger Sherman (signature)

ROGER SHERMAN (Connecticut; 1721–1793)
Strict Puritan ▪ Shoemaker ▪ Lawyer ▪ Legislator ▪ Only person to sign Articles of Association, Declaration of Independence, Articles of Confederation, and the Constitution ▪ Mayor, New Haven (1784–1793) ▪ U.S.

Representative ▪ U.S. Senator ▪ Treasurer, benefactor, Yale College ▪ Proposed dual system of representation in Congress

Jaʃ Smithn

JAMES SMITH (Pennsylvania; 1713–1806)
Emigrated, Ireland (1727) ▪ Surveyor ▪ Lawyer ▪ Iron manufacturer ▪ Colonel, Pennsylvania militia ▪ Congressman

Rich Stockton

RICHARD STOCKTON (New Jersey; 1730–1781)
An "independent soul" ▪ First in class, College of New Jersey, and a lifelong financial advisor ▪ Cultivated lawyer ▪ Unsuccessful candidate for governor of New Jersey (1776) ▪ Declined election to Chief Justiceship, Supreme Court, New Jersey, in order to remain in Congress ▪ Invalided by harsh British imprisonment ▪ Champion of law and order ▪ Bred horses and cattle at his extensive landed estate

Geo Taylor

GEORGE TAYLOR (Pennsylvania; 1716–1781)
Emigrated, Ireland (1736) ▪ Justice of the Peace ▪ Iron manufacturer ▪ Not present for debate on Declaration of Independence, but signatory

Thos Stone

THOMAS STONE (Maryland;1743–1787)
Conservative ▪ Lawyer ▪ Congressman (1775–1776; 1778; 1784) ▪ Maryland Senate (1779–1783) ▪ Long but limited political career

Matthew Thornton

MATTHEW THORNTON (New Hampshire; 1714–1803)

"An Honest Man," emigrated, Ireland (1718) ▪ Farmer ▪ Grandson of a propriety governor ▪ Militia colonel, New Hampshire militia, Revolutionary War ▪ Several years in Congress ▪ Literary ambitions

Geo Walton

GEORGE WALTON (Georgia; 1749–1804)

Orphan, self-taught ▪ Apprentice to a carpenter ▪ Imperious Secretary, Provincial Congress (1775) ▪ British prisoner for nearly two years during Revolutionary War ▪ Georgia governor ▪ Negotiated treaties with the Cherokee and with the Iroquois ▪ Chief Justice, Georgia (1789) ▪ U.S. Senator

Wm Whipple

WILLIAM WHIPPLE (New Hampshire; 1730–1785)

Spirited patriot ▪ Freed his slaves ▪ Soldier, Revolutionary War ▪ Delegate, Provincial Congress (1775) ▪ Judge, New Hampshire Supreme Court (1782)

Wm Williams

WILLIAM WILLIAMS (Connecticut; 1731–1811)

Theology student, Harvard (1751) ▪ Soldier, expedition to Lake George (1755) ▪ Member, Council of Safety, Revolutionary War ▪ Vigorous pen

James Wilson

JAMES WILSON (Pennsylvania; 1742–1798)

Studied in Scotland, where born, emigrated (1765) ▪ First law professor, College of Philadelphia ▪ Powerful logician, his mind "a blaze of light" ▪ Associate U.S. justice, nine years ▪ Significant framer of the Constitution (1787) ▪ Buffeted by financial storms ▪ Inept land speculation prompted flight to North Carolina to avoid creditors

Jno Witherspoon

JOHN WITHERSPOON (New Jersey; 1723–1794)
Born Scotland ▪ Graduate, Edinburgh University (1739) ▪ President, College of New Jersey (now Princeton University) ▪ Only active clergyman to sign Declaration of Independence ▪ Unrivaled position in American ecclesiastical circles ▪ Believed country in danger of rotting for want of independence ▪ Sat in New Jersey provincial assemblies under local committees of correspondence ▪ Was in Congress until 1782 ▪ Believed proper use of English important in development of United States ▪ Signed Articles of Confederation ▪ Fathered ten children ▪ Blind last ten years of life ▪ Served in Congress 1776–1782

Oliver Wolcott

OLIVER WOLCOTT (Connecticut; 1726–1797)
First in class, Yale college, four years ▪ Youngest of fifteen children ▪ Commissioner, Indian Affairs ▪ Commander, Connecticut regiments ▪ Governor, Connecticut, one year ▪ Staunch Federalist

George Wythe

GEORGE WYTHE (Virginia; 1726–1806)
Name rhymes with Smithe ▪ Masters Latin, Greek ▪ Lawyer ▪ First law professorship, College of William and Mary ▪ Member, clerk, House of Burgesses (1758–1768) ▪ Chancellor, Virginia (1778) ▪ Poisoned by a grandnephew

Addendum

Four delegates, including John Dickinson, who held political posts in Delaware *and* Pennsylvania, refused to sign the Declaration of Independence and resigned from Congress. Three others refused to sign the Declaration and also resigned from Congress: Charles Humphreys, Thomas Willing, and John Alsop. Seven delegates were not present in Congress on July 4 but signed later: Thomas Heyward, Jr., Thomas McKean, Elbridge

Gerry, Samuel Chase, George Wythe, Richard Henry Lee, and Richard Stockton. Most of the delegates signed the document, engrossed on parchment, on August 2, and toasted the event with the colonists' favorite wine, Maderia.

Twenty-four of the signers were lawyers and jurists. Eleven were merchants. Nine were farmers and plantation owners. Thomas McKean, of Delaware, didn't put his name to the document until 1781. Five of the signatories were captured by the British and tortured. They had known that the penalty could be death if captured. Nine of the signatories fought in the Revolutionary War and died of wounds or hardship.

The States are Paramount

Delegates of the thirteen states of the nascent United States of America wrote the first U.S. constitution—the Articles of Confederation—a year after the Declaration of Independence. The former English colonies were to form a league of friendship, a loose but perpetual union, more of a diplomatic body than a direct government. The states were paramount—the sovereign, disunited, selfish, feuding states. The president was a figurehead. The one-chamber Congress was the central government but subordinate to the states. Each state, regardless of population, had one vote. Congressional action on critical problems required approval of nine states—a hamstringing situation. It took the states four years (1777–1781) to ratify the feckless, states-oriented charter. In 1787, the states threw out the Articles and composed the Constitution, the supreme laws of the land.

The Articles of Confederation (1777):

To all to whom these Presents shall come, we the undersigned Delegates of the States affixed to our Names send greeting.

Whereas the Delegates of the United States of America in Congress assembled did on the fifteenth day of November in the Year of our Lord One Thousand Seven Hundred and Seventy-seven, and in the Second Year of the Independence of America agree to certain articles of Confederation and perpetual Union between the States of Newhampshire, Massachusetts-bay, Rhodeisland and Providence Plantations, Connecticut, New York, New Jersey, Pennsylvania, Delaware, Maryland, Virginia, North-Carolina, South-Carolina and Georgia in the Words following, viz. "Articles of Confederation and perpetual Union between the States of Newhampshire, Massachusetts-bay, Rhodeisland and Providence Plantations, Connecticut, New-York, New-Jersey, Pennsylvania, Delaware, Maryland, Virginia, North-Carolina, South-Carolina and Georgia."

Article I. The Stile of this confederacy shall be "The United States of America."

Article II. Each state retains its sovereignty, freedom and independence, and every Power, Jurisdiction and right, which is not by this confederation expressly delegated to the United States, in Congress assembled.

Article III. The said states hereby severally enter into a firm league of friendship with each other, for their common defense, the security of their Liberties, and their mutual and general welfare, binding themselves to assist each other, against all force offered to, or attacks made upon them, or any of them, on account of religion, sovereignty, trade or any other pretence whatever.

Article IV. The better to secure and perpetuate mutual friendship and intercourse among the people of the different states in this union, the free inhabitants of each of these states, paupers, vagabonds and fugitives from Justice excepted, shall be entitled to all privileges and immunities of free citizens in the several states; and the people of each state shall have free ingress and regress to and from any other state, and shall enjoy therein all the privileges of trade and commerce, subject to the same duties, impositions and restrictions as the inhabitants thereof respectively, provided that such restriction shall not extend so far as to prevent the removal of property imported into any state, to any other state of which the Owner is an inhabitant; provided also that no imposition, duties or restriction shall be laid by any state, on the property of the united states, or either of them.

If any Person guilty of, or charged with treason, felony, or other high misdemeanor in any state, shall flee from justice, and be found in any of the united states, he shall upon demand of the Governor or executive power, of the state from which he fled, be delivered up and removed to the state having jurisdiction of his offence.

Full faith and credit shall be given in each of these states to the records, acts and judicial proceedings of the courts and magistrates of every other state.

Article V. For the more convenient management of the general interests of the united states, delegates shall be annually appointed in such manner as the legislature of each state shall direct, to meet in Congress on the first Monday in November, in every year, with a power reserved to each state, to recall its delegates, or any of them, at any time within the year, and to send others in their stead, for the remainder of the Year.

No state shall be represented in Congress by less than two, nor by more than seven Members; and no person shall be capable of being a delegate for more than three years in any term of six years; nor shall any person, being a delegate, be capable of holding any office under the united states, for which he, or another for his benefit receives any salary, fees or emolument of any kind.

Each state shall maintain its own delegates in a meeting of the states, and while they act as members of the committee of the states.

In determining questions in the united states, in Congress assembled, each state shall have one vote.

Freedom of speech and debate in Congress shall not be impeached or questioned in any Court, or place out of Congress, and the members of congress shall be protected in their persons from arrests and imprisonments, during the time of their going to and from, and attendance on congress, except for treason, felony, or breach of the peace.

Article VI. No state without the Consent of the united states in congress assembled, shall send any embassy to, or receive any embassy from, or enter into any conference, agreement, alliance or treaty with any King, prince or state; nor shall any person holding any office of profit or trust under the united states, or any of them, accept of any present, emolument, office or title of any kind whatever from any king, prince or foreign state, nor shall the united states in congress assembled, or any of them, grant any title of nobility.

No two or more states shall enter into any treaty, confederation or alliance whatever between them, without the consent of the united states in congress assembled, specifying accurately the purposes for which the same is to be entered into, and how long it shall continue.

No state shall lay any imposts or duties, which may interfere with any stipulations in treaties, entered into by the united states in congress assembled, with any king, prince or state, in pursuance of any treaties already proposed by congress, to the courts of France and Spain.

No vessels of war shall be kept up in time of peace by any state, except such number only, as shall be deemed necessary by the united states in congress assembled, for the defence of such state, or its trade; nor shall any body of forces be kept up by any state, in time of peace, except such number only, as in the judgment of the united states, in congress assembled, shall be deemed requisite to garrison the forts necessary for the defence of such state; but every state shall always keep up a well regulated and disciplined militia, sufficiently armed and accoutred, and shall provide and constantly have ready for use, in public stores, a due number of field pieces and tents, and a proper quantity of arms, ammunition and camp equipage.

No state shall engage in any war without the consent of the united states in congress assembled, unless such state be actually invaded by enemies, or shall have received certain advice of a resolution being formed by some nation of Indians to invade such state, and the danger is so imminent as not to admit of a delay, till the united states in congress assembled can be consulted: nor shall any state grant commissions to any ships or vessels of war, nor letters of marque or reprisal, except it be after a declaration of war by the united states in congress assembled, and then only against the kingdom or state and the subjects thereof, against which war has been so declared, and under such regulations as shall be established by the united states in congress assembled, unless such state be infested by pirates, in which case vessels of war may be fitted out for that occasion, and kept so long as the danger shall continue, or until the united states in congress assembled shall determine otherwise.

Article VII. When land-forces are raised by any state of the common defence, all officers of or under the rank of colonel, shall be appointed by the legislature of each state respectively by whom such forces shall be raised, or in such manner as such state shall direct, and all vacancies shall be filled up by the state which first made the appointment.

Article VIII. All charges of war, and all other expences that shall be incurred for the common defence or general welfare, and allowed by the united states in congress assembled, shall be defrayed out of a common treasury, which shall be supplied by the several states, in proportion to the value of all land within each state, granted to or surveyed for any Person, as such land and the buildings and improvements thereon shall be estimated according to such mode as the united states in congress assembled, shall from time to time direct and appoint. The taxes for paying that proportion shall be laid and levied by the authority and direction of the legislatures of the several states within the time agreed upon by the united states in congress assembled.

Article IX. The united states in congress assembled, shall have the sole and exclusive right and power of determining on peace and war, except in the cases mentioned in the sixth article—of sending and receiving ambassadors—entering into treaties and alliances, provided that no treaty of commerce shall be made whereby the legislative power of the respective states shall be restrained from imposing such imposts and duties on foreigners, as their own people are subjected to, or from prohibiting the exportation or importation of and species of goods or commodities whatsoever—of establishing rules for deciding in all cases, what captures on land or water shall be legal, and in what manner prizes taken by land or naval forces in the service of the united states shall be divided or appropriated—of granting letters of marque and reprisal in times of peace—appointing courts for the trial of piracies and felonies committed on the high seas and establishing courts for receiving and determining finally appeals in all cases of captures, provided that no member of congress shall be appointed a judge of any of the said courts.

The united states in congress assembled shall also be the last resort on appeal in all disputes and differences now subsisting or that thereafter may arise between two or more states concerning boundary, jurisdiction or any other cause whatever; which authority shall always be exercised in the manner following. Whenever the legislative or executive authority or lawful agent of any state in controversy with another shall present a petition to congress stating the matter in question and praying for a hearing, notice thereof shall be given by order of congress to the legislative or executive authority of the other state in controversy, and a day assigned for the appearance of the parties by their lawful agents, who shall then be directed to appoint by joint consent, commissioners or judges to constitute a court for hearing and determining the matter in question: but if they cannot agree, congress shall name three persons out of each of the united states, and from the list of such persons each party shall alternately strike out one, the petitioners beginning, until the number shall be reduced to thirteen; and from that number not less than seven, nor more than nine names as congress shall direct, shall in the presence of congress be drawn out by lot, and the persons whose names shall be so drawn or any five of them, shall be commissioners or judges, to hear and finally determine the controversy, so always as a major part of the judges who shall hear the cause shall agree in the determination: and if either party shall neglect to attend at the day appointed, without shewing reasons, which congress shall judge sufficient, or being present shall refuse to strike, the congress shall proceed to nominate three persons out of each state, and the secretary of congress shall strike in behalf of such party absent or refusing; and the judgment and sentence of the court to be appointed, in the manner before prescribed, shall be final and conclusive; and if any of the parties shall refuse to submit to the authority of such court, or to appear or defend their claim or cause, the court shall nevertheless proceed to pronounce sentence, or judgment, which shall in like manner be final and decisive, the judgment or sentence and other proceedings being in either case transmitted to congress, and lodged among the acts of congress for the security of the parties concerned: provided that every commissioner, before he sits in judgment, shall take an oath to be administered by one of the judges of the supreme or superior court of the state, where the cause shall be tried, "well and truly to hear and determine the matter in question, according to the best of his judgment, without favour, affection or hope of reward:" provided also that no state shall be deprived of territory for the benefit of the united states.

All controversies concerning the private right of soil claimed under different grants of two or more states, whose jurisdictions as they may respect such lands, and the states which passed such grants are adjusted, the said grants or either of them being at the same time claimed to have originated antecedent to such settlement of jurisdiction, shall on the petition of either party to the congress of the united states, be finally determined as near as maybe in the same manner as is before prescribed for deciding disputes respecting territorial jurisdictions between different states.

The united states in congress assembled shall also have the sole and exclusive right and power of regulating the alloy and value of coin struck by their own authority, or by that of the respective states—fixing the standard of weights and measures throughout the united states—regulating the trade and managing all affairs with the Indians, not members of any of the states, provided that the legislative right of any state within its own limits be not infringed or violated—establishing and regulating post-offices from one state to another, throughout all of the united states, and exacting such postage on the papers passing thro' the same as may be requisite to defray the expences of the said office—appointing all officers of the land forces, in the service of the united states, excepting regimental officers—appointing all the officers of the naval forces, and commissioning all officers whatever in the service of the united states—making rules for the government and regulation of the said land and naval forces, and directing their operations.

The united states in congress assembled shall have authority to appoint a committee, to sit in the recess of congress, to be denominated "A Committee of the States," and to consist of one delegate from each state; and to appoint such other committees and civil officers as may be necessary for managing the general affairs of the united states under their direction—to appoint one of their number to preside, provided that no person be allowed to serve in the office of president more than one year in any term of three years; to ascertain the necessary sums of Money to be raised for the service of the united states, and to appropriate and apply the same for defraying the public expences—to borrow money, or emit bills on the credit of the united states, transmitting every half year to the respective states an account of the sums of money so borrowed or emitted,—to build and equip a navy—to agree upon the number of land forces, and to make requisitions from each State for its quota, in proportion to the number of white inhabitants in such state; which requisition shall be binding, and thereupon the legislature of each state shall appoint the regimental officers, raise the men and cloath, arm and equip them in a soldier like manner, at the expence of the united states, and the officers and men so cloathed, armed and equipped shall march to the place appointed, and within the time agreed on by the united states in congress assembled: But if the united states in congress assembled shall, on consideration of circumstances judge proper that any state should not raise men, or should raise a smaller number than its quota, and that any other state should raise a greater number of men than the quota thereof, such extra number shall be raised, officered, cloathed, armed and equipped in the same manner as the quota of such state, unless the legislature of such state shall judge that such extra number cannot be safely spared out of the same, in which case they shall raise officer, cloath, arm and equip as many of such extra number as they judge can be safely spared. And the officers and men so cloathed, armed and equipped, shall march to the place appointed, and within the time agreed on by the united states in congress assembled.

The united states in congress assembled shall never engage in a war, nor grant letters of marque and reprisal in time of peace, nor enter into any treaties or alliances, nor coin money, nor regulate the value thereof, nor ascertain the sums and expences necessary for the defence and welfare of the united states, or any of them, nor emit bills, nor borrow money on the credit of the united states, nor appropriate money, nor agree upon the number of vessels of war, to be built or purchased, or the number of land or sea forces to be raised, nor appoint a commander in chief of the army or navy, unless nine states assent to the same: nor shall a question on any other point, except for adjourning from day to day be determined, unless by the votes of a majority of the united states in congress assembled.

The congress of the united states shall have power to adjourn to any time within the year, and to any place within the united states, so that no period of adjournment be for a longer duration than the space of six Months, and shall publish the Journal of their proceedings monthly, except such parts thereof relating to treaties, alliances or military operations, as in their judgment require secresy; and the yeas and nays of the delegates of each state on any question shall be entered on the Journal, when it is desired by any delegate; and the delegates of a state, or any of them, at his or their request shall be furnished with a transcript of the said Journal, except such parts as are above excepted, to lay before the Legislatures of the several states.

Article X. The committee of the states, or any nine of them, shall be authorized to execute, in the recess of congress, such of the powers of congress as the united states in congress assembled, by the consent of nine states, shall from time to time think expedient to vest them with; provided that no power be delegated to the said committee, for the exercise of which, by the articles of confederation, the voice of nine states in the congress of the united states assembled is requisite.

Article XI. Canada acceding to this confederation, and joining in the measures of the united states, shall be admitted into, and entitled to all the advantages of this union: but no other colony shall be admitted into the same, unless such admission be agreed to by nine states.

Article XII. All bills of credit emitted, monies borrowed and debts contracted by, or under the authority of congress, before the assembling of the united states, in pursuance of the present confederation, shall be deemed and considered as a charge against the united states, for payment and satisfaction whereof the said united states, and the public faith are hereby solemnly pledged.

Article XIII. Every state shall abide by the determinations of the united states in congress assembled, on all questions which by this confederation are submitted to them. And the Articles of this confederation shall be inviolably observed by every state, and the union shall be perpetual; nor shall any alteration at any time hereafter be made in any of them; unless such alteration be agreed to in a congress of the united states, and be afterwards confirmed by the legislatures of every state.

And WHEREAS it hath pleased the Great Governor of the World to incline the hearts of the legislatures we respectively represent in congress, to approve of, and to authorize us to ratify the said articles of confederation and perpetual union. KNOW

Ye that we [the undersigned delegates], by virtue of the power and authority to us given for that purpose, do by these presents, in the name and in behalf of our respective constituents, full and entirely ratify and confirm each and every of the said articles of confederation and perpetual union, and all and singular the matters and things therein contained: And we do further solemnly plight and engage the faith of our respective constituents, that they shall abide by the determinations of the united states in congress assembled, on all questions, which by the said confederation are submitted to them. And that the articles thereof shall be inviolably observed by the states we respectively represent, and that the union shall be perpetual.

In Witness whereof we have hereunto set our hands in Congress. Done at Philadelphia in the state of Pennsylvania the ninth Day of July in the Year of our Lord one Thousand seven Hundred and Seventy-eight, and in the third year of the independence of America.

The Original Thirteen

The original thirteen states—England's American colonies before independence was declared in 1776, have prospered over the centuries:

Connecticut

Connecticut ("He Who Transplanted Still Sustains"), the southernmost of the six New England states, the third-smallest state in area, the wealthiest per person. In 1639, three towns formed an English colony after trouncing Pequot Indians resisting white settlement. They adopted the first written constitution based on consent of the governed, the Fundamental Orders. In 1662, England granted the colony land stretching all the way (as it turned out) to the Pacific Ocean. Connecticut held the claim for more than a century, then assigned the land to the new Federal government. Sir Edmund Andros tried to carry out King James II's mandate to lump five colonies together: Plymouth, Massachusetts Bay, Connecticut, New Haven, and New Hampshire. In 1687, Connecticut's colonists defied the governor-general of the Dominion of New England. Connecticut refused to surrender its liberal royal charter, hiding the document in the hollow of a white oak tree in Hartford, the celebrated Charter Oak. (The 1,000-year-old tree fell on August 21, 1856.) For 174 years, the colony and then the state had two capitals, the cities of Hartford and New Haven, which are about thirty-five miles apart.

Four delegates from Connecticut signed the Declaration of Independence.

Delaware

Delaware ("Liberty and Independence"), the second smallest state in area in the U.S. and the fifth smallest in population, was renamed for the first governor of the colony of Virginia, Thomas West, Baron de Warr. Dutchmen were the first European settlers. They arrived in 1631 and were massacred by American Indians. In 1638, Swedes established New Sweden, the first permanent settlement in the Delaware River valley, and built the first log cabins in North America. New Sweden competed in trading furs with the Dutch settlement of New Amsterdam. In 1655, a Dutch fleet commanded by Peter Stuyvesant, director-general of New Amsterdam, subdued New Sweden. Nine years later, the peg-legged Stuyvesant surrendered Dutch holdings in the region to English authority. In the mid-1700s, Delaware was linked with Pennsylvania. For a time, Delaware was a slave state. It was the first state to adopt the Constitution (1787), but it did not ratify the three Civil War-amendments to the Constitution abolishing slavery, making black people citizens, and giving blacks the right to vote.

Three delegates from Delaware signed the Declaration of Independence.

Georgia

Georgia ("Agriculture and Commerce"), the largest state east of the Mississippi River, was the first Southern state to approve the new constitution of the United States. Many flags have flown over the region: those of Spain, France, pirates, Great Britain, the United States, and the Confederacy. Georgia was the last British colony founded in America before the Revolution. The English philanthropist James Oglethorpe, who established the colony, named Georgia for King George II, who in 1732 had granted the colony a twenty-one-year charter. Englishmen fleeing religious persecution found a haven in Georgia. Oglethorpe served as leader of the colony (he never was governor, contrary to popular histories), ruling by strength of personality. Three decades before the Revolution, Oglethorpe, allied with Creek Indians, defeated Spanish troops in the Battle of Bloody Marsh, on St. Simons Island, effectively ending Spain's claim to.the region. During the Revolutionary War, the British captured every important community in Georgia. Georgia voted to leave the Union three months before the Civil War erupted.

Three delegates from Georgia signed the Declaration of Independence.

Maryland

Maryland ("Strong Deeds, Gentle Words") has been described as America in miniature. The description alludes to the state's geography: forested mountains, rolling farmlands, spongy swamps, wide sandy beaches, dramatic cliffs. Although all of Maryland's lakes are artificial, Chesapeake Bay is the largest bay in the nation: 195 miles long, cutting Maryland nearly in half. Maryland was named for Queen Henrietta Maria, wife of England's King Charles I. The colony was a haven for persecuted Catholics. The capital city, Annapolis, originally called Providence, was settled in 1649 by Puritans fleeing Virginia. Conflicts all but destroyed religious freedom, which had been guaranteed. In 1654, Puritans repealed legislation for toleration; there was much anti-Catholic activity. The seaport settlement of Baltimore, founded in 1739, was named for Baron Baltimore, Charles Calvert. The city was the seat of the first Roman Catholic archdiocese in the United States. Maryland was nicknamed "the Old Line State" when its troops of the line won General George Washington's praise during the

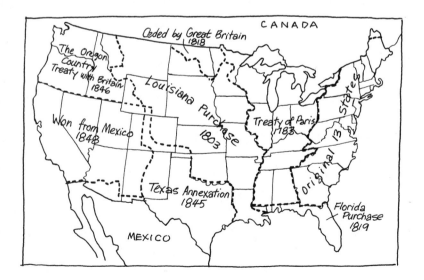

Revolutionary War. Annapolis was the U.S. capital for nearly a year. Delegates to the Annapolis Convention (1786) called for the Federal Convention, which composed the Constitution (1787), in Philadelphia. In 1791, Maryland ceded land to the U.S. for the District of Columbia, the permanent U.S. capital. The lyrics for the U.S. anthem, set to the tune of an English drinking song, were composed by a young lawyer, Francis Scott Key, in Baltimore harbor after the British bombardment of a fort there during the War of 1812.

Four delegates from Maryland signed the Declaration of Independence.

Massachusetts

Massachusetts ("By the Sword We Seek Peace, But Peace Only Under Liberty") led the colonies' resistance to British policies in the 1760s and 1770s. The colony of Massachusetts-Bay was much larger than the state of Massachusetts; New Hampshire and Maine were part of the colony. Algonquian Indians called the Massachuset gave their name to the region. Whalers, fishermen, and explorers were the first European arrivals. In December 1773, several American patriots donned Indian disguises, boarded three tea ships of the British East Indian Company in Boston harbor, and threw 340 casks of low-priced tea into the water; the Boston Tea Party protested Parliament's claim that it could tax the colonies and protected colonial merchants' lucrative source of revenue. Fourteen months later, the American Revolution began in the Massachusetts villages of Lexington and Concord, near Boston. "Upon a very good horse," superpatriot Paul Revere warned households along the road from Boston to the Middlesex countryside that British troops were on the march, searching for illegally stored munitions. Thirteen months before the thirteen English colonies declared independence, British forces drove back colonial militia in Boston; the Americans' heroic fight however, stiffened colonial morale, as well as their resolve to be free of British rule. In the 1780s, a former Continental Army captain, Daniel Shays, and discontended farmers and tradesmen in the western part of Massachusetts took up muskets, staves, and pitchforks against local authorities, and defended homes and families against foreclosure and imprisonment for debt. Shay's Rebellion spread, and hastened the creation of a strong national government capable of dealing with disorder (and order).

Four delegates from Massachusetts signed the Declaration of Independence.

New Hampshire

("Live Free or Die") A former governor of Newfoundland and other Englishmen were granted lands that became the earliest settled part of New Hampshire, the Granite State. The lands included part of the future state of Maine. New Hampshire, named for a county in England, became a British royal province in 1679. Seven years later, New Hampshire became the first of the thirteen British colonies in North America to establish its own government. Its western boundary was settled in 1791 when neighboring Vermont was admitted to the Union as the fourteenth state. The nation's oldest building in which the state legislature meets in original chambers is the state house in Concord. Mount Washington sits squarely in the path of storm systems. It was at its summit that the highest wind speed on the planet was registered: 231 miles per hour.

Three delegates from New Hampshire signed the Declaration of Independence.

New Jersey

New Jersey ("Liberty and Prosperity") is the fourth smallest state and the most crowded with more than 1,000 people per square mile. (New Jersey today is more densely populated than India or Japan.) The New Jersey Turnpike is the most traveled road in the fifty states. New Jersey was settled by Dutchmen and Swedes, and was part of Dutch New Netherlands. English troops conquered Dutch settlements in 1664 The Middle Atlantic colony was named for the English Channel island of Jersey. For a brief time, "New Jersey" was divided into two colonies, East Jersey and West Jersey. During the Revolutionary War, American and British soldiers fought nearly 100 battles in New Jersey. The Frenchman who laid out the District of Columbia designed the New Jersey city of Paterson, north of Newark, at the 770-foot high Great Falls of the Passaic River; Paterson became a model for Treasury Secretary Alexander Hamilton's encouragement of American industry. The first dinosaur skeleton found in North America was unearthed in Haddonfield, in 1858.

Five delegates from New Jersey signed the Declaration of Independence.

New York

New York ("Ever Upward") was the first future state to be observed by a European (Christopher Columbus apparently never saw the North American mainland). In 1524, Giovanni de Verrazano, an Italian in the service of France, sailed into New York Harbor searching for a westward passage to the Orient. He flew the fleur-de-lis, emblem of France's royal family. Verrazano, was from a long line of bankers and importers, and had lived in Egypt and Syria. He learned navigation in the Levantine Basin. It was springtime when Verrazano's white caravel, the three-masted *Dauphine*, named for the French crown prince, eased at night before a soft southwest wind into the Narrows between the west end of New York's Long Island and southeastern Staten Island. He saw "people, similar to the others, clothed with the feathers of birds of various colors. . . . a pleasant place . . . below steep little hills. And from among those hills a great stream of water ran into the sea. . . . we rode at anchor in a spot well guarded from the wind, and we passed into the river with *Dauphine*'s little boat," or shallop. In the distance were the sounds of drums and rattles. The imperious Verrazano "baptized" the region and its harbor, naming them Angouleme, honoring a duchy created by King Francis I. In 1609, another European, Henry Hudson, an Englishman in the service of Holland, entered New York Harbor, then sailed north on the Hudson River for 150 miles, as far as Albany, site of the state capital today. In 1626, the Dutch West India Company purchased the island of Manhattan from the Canarsie Indians for about $24 worth of trinkets. New York was named, in 1685, for the Duke of York, who became England's King James II.

Four delegates from New York signed the Declaration of Independence.

North Carolina

("To Be Rather Than to Seem") It was along the coast that the English quite naturally first attempted to colonize the "new world." In the 1580s, Sir Walter Raleigh directed expeditions to Roanoke Island. The first child born of English parents in America, Virginia Dare, was born on Roanoke, August 18, 1587. All of Roanoke's settlers disappeared mysteriously; to this day, they are known as "the lost colony." North Carolina once was united with South Carolina. The territory was called Carolina, for Kings Charles I and Charles II, of England. (In Latin, Charles is spelled *Carolus*.) It was in the early 1700s that the British separated the region into the provinces of North Carolina and South Carolina.

The first organized defiance of British law by Americans occurred in North Carolina, in 1774. Fifty-one women in the town of Edenton resolved not to drink tea or wear clothing made in the "Mother Country" until England's tax on tea was repealed—the Edenton Tea Party. North Carolina was the first English colony to authorize its delegates in the Second Continental Congress to vote for independence. But not until George Washington had been president for more than seven months did North Carolina join other states in ratifying the Constitution.

Three delegates from North Carolina signed the Declaration of Independence.

Pennsylvania

Pennsylvania ("Virtue, Liberty, and Independence") is known as the Keystone State, because its keystone, or strategic, geographical location was at the midpoint of the original thirteen states. Like the keystone of an arch, Pennsylvania held together the states to the north and those to the south. Many notable battles were fought in Pennsylvania during the War for Independence. It was in Pennsylvania's largest city, Philadelphia (population 28,522 in the first U.S. census in 1790), the City of Brotherly Love, that America's two founding documents, the Declaration of Independence (1776) and the Constitution (1787), were drafted, debated, and promulgated. Philadelphia was the second capital of the United States (1790–1800). Pennsylvania was not named for its founder, a Quaker leader, William Penn; it was named for his father. In Latin, Pennsylvania—

Penn plus *silvanus*—is "Penn's Woods." Fifty-eight percent of the state is forested. William Penn proclaimed the colony a "holy experiment"; everyone would be welcomed, and they could live and worship in freedom. It was in Philadelphia, in 1775, that the first society in America dedicated to abolishing slavery was formed.

Nine delegates from Pennsylvania signed the Declaration of Independence.

Rhode Island

Despite its name, Rhode Island ("Hope") is not an island. It may have taken its name from Rhode Island, an island in nearby Narragansett Bay. Always the smallest state in area, Rhode Island has the longest official name: State of Rhode Island and Providence Plantations (Its settlements sometimes were called plantations.) "Little Rhodey" is only 37 miles east-west and only 48 miles north-south. (Four hundred and seventy-five Rhode Islands could fit into Alaska, the largest of today's fifty states.) It was founded by refugees seeking religious and political freedom. The first settlements were established by dissenters banished by Puritans from the colony of Massachusetts Bay; the dissenters believed that no person should be persecuted by civil authorities for religious beliefs; everyone could worship God in his or her own way. (Separation of church and state became a guiding principle of the United States.) A dissenter named Roger Williams founded the town called Providence, so named because, Williams said, God's providence, or hand, had led him there. The first Baptist Church was built in Providence. The oldest synagogue in the U.S. is in Newport. The state did not send a delegation to the Constitutional Convention (1787); its rural legislators wanted no interference with their policy of printing paper money to inflate the currency and drive down the value of debts. Other states denounced Rhode Island's policy as fatal to sound credit. Conservatives in the adjoining states of Massachusetts and Connecticut wanted to strike Rhode Island out of the Union and share its space. Rhode Island did not ratify the Constitution until May 1790; when it did, it did by only two votes.

Two delegates from Rhode Island signed the Declaration of Independence.

South Carolina

South Carolina ("While I Breathe, I Hope") was home to about fifty Indian nations in the early 1600s: the Cherokee, Yamasee, and Catawba were the principal nations. During the 1700s, the port of Charleston was a vital link with the West Indies; it was part of the America-Africa "triangle trade" route: molasses and sugar were shipped from the West Indies to America and made into rum, which was shipped to Africa, where it was traded for slaves, who were sold in the West Indies for molasses and sugar. At one time, the black population in the region was nearly twice that of the white population. The important cash crops were rice and indigo. After the American Revolution, cotton became king and plantation owners ran the state. During the War of Independence, at least 2,000 battles and skirmishes were waged in South Carolina; about eighty years later, South Carolina was the first of eleven southern states to secede from the Union. It left a month after Abraham Lincoln had been elected the sixteenth president.

Four delegates from South Carolina signed the Declaration of Independence.

Virginia

Virginia ("Thus Always to Tyrants"), once the largest state, was in the forefront of freedom from Great Britain and in organizing the government of the United States. Virginia once included the present-day states of Kentucky, which split off from Virginia in 1792, and West Virginia, which broke away in 1861. (Virginia is the only state to produce two other states.) The state's Founding Fathers included George Washington, first president and the army commander who defeated the British in the Revolutionary War; Thomas Jefferson, author of the Declaration of Independence, second vice president, and third president; James Madison, fourth president, third vice president, "father of the Constitution"; James Monroe, fourth vice president, fifth president; John Marshall, first chief justice of the United States; Patrick Henry and Richard Henry Lee, who argued vociferously for American independence (1776) and a Bill of Rights (1791), and George Mason, whose Declaration of Rights for Virginia became a model for the U.S. Bill of Rights (the first ten amendments to the Constitution) and for bills of rights around the world. In October 1781, six years after "Lexington and Concord," the British surrendered in Virginia to American forces. Virginia was named for Queen Elizabeth I, England's "Virgin Queen." Two years after the Constitution was framed, Virginia, as Maryland had done, ceded lands for creation of the U.S. capital city.

Seven delegates from Virginia signed the Declaration of Independence.

War for Independence

IT TOOK MORE THAN SIX YEARS FOR AMERICAN FORCES TO WIN THE WAR OF INDEPENDENCE. The first shots were fired more than a year before America even declared its independence from Britain. They were fired on April 19, 1775, in the Massachusetts villages of Lexington (on the town common) and Concord (at North Bridge). Vermont's Ethan Allen and his Green Mountain Boys captured New York's Fort Ticonderoga on Lake Champlain; two days later, Seth Warner captured nearby Crown Point. Congress named George Washington commander-in-chief of the American army. The general hoped the Declaration of Independence would be a "fresh incentive to every officer and soldier . . . knowing that now the peace and safety of his country depends (under God) solely on the success

of our arms." The Declaration of Independence raised rebel morale. The British tried to negotiate a peace.

The end came years later, in Virginia. American forces and French allies bottled up British troops on a peninsula there.

Some of the headline events during the long war: Virginia's royal governor orders bombardment of Norfolk, Virginia . . . British soldiers try to seize munitions in Salem, Mass., the

"Salem Bridge Alarm."... British troops evacuate New York City... Patriots defeat Tories in North Carolina... The Boston Massacre... Parliament repeals Stamp Act... General Washington fortifies Dorchester Heights... Customs collectors seize John Hancock's ship... British forces occupy Boston... Virginia's governor dissolves House of Burgesses, but delegates meet privately to declare boycott on dutiable goods... Parliament repeals Townshend Act, but maintains tax on tea, symbolic of Parliament's insistence on right to impose taxes on colonists... Second Continental Congress gathers in Philadelphia... Colonists send grievances to King George III... Patriots seize gunpowder in Savannah, Georgia... Colonial frontiersmen massacre Indians in West Virginia... British General Thomas Gage arrives in Boston as vice admiral and royal governor of Massachusetts-Bay colony... Colonial anger prompts radicals, disguised as Indians, to throw 342 chests of tea off ships into harbor, the Boston Tea Party... Paul Revere warns Massachusetts minutemen that the British army was coming... Parliament passes "Intolerable Acts" to punish Massachusetts colonists for Tea Party; closes Boston port until payment is made for destroyed tea. Colonists are forced to quarter British soldiers, and are deprived of many rights... Patriots

generaled by Benedict Arnold raid St. John's, Canada... British fleet shells Bristol, Rhode Island... Patriots capture British schooner near Boston... Mass. militia captures Fort William and Mary, near Portsmouth... Patrick Henry, of Virginia, denounces British rule, declares, "Give me liberty or give me death."... Green Mountain Boys at gateway to Lake Champlain and water route to Canada... British generals arrive in Boston... Patriots raid British munitions at Turtle Bay, New York... Patriots defeat British in Maine... British declare martial law in Canada... Patriots break British blockade of Boston Harbor (June 13, 1776)... Continental Congress adopts Stars and Stripes as official U.S. flag... Major General Gates commands American forces in North... A Washington bodyguard is found guilty of mutiny and sedition, and is hanged... British defeat rebels at Bunker Hill, in Boston... Washington arrives in Cambridge, Mass.... Congress adopts Declaration of the Causes and Necessities of Taking Up Arms... Patriots capture Fort Charlotte, South Carolina... Americans capture British vessel off Tybee Island, Georgia... Patriots defeat British in second raid on Great Brewster Island, Massachusetts... King George claims Americans are in open, avowed rebellion... Americans invade Quebec... Patriots occupy Fort Johnson, South Carolina... Patriots capture British supply train in Canada... Congress authorizes acquisition of first warships.... Patriots defeat British in Virginia, whose royal governor declares martial law... George Sackville, Lord Germain, is appointed British Secretary of State for the Colonies... Patriots capture Montreal... Tories defeat rebels in skirmish at Ninety Six, South Carolina... England recalls General Gage, names Sir William Howe commander-in-chief of British forces in North America... Americans and Indian nations meet in Pittsburgh conference (September 26, 1775)... British burn Falmouth, Maine... John Paul Jones raises first Continental Union flag.... Patriots bombard Quebec and under Colonel Henry Knox

leave Fort Ticonderoga with captured cannon for siege of Boston ... Virginia convention instructs its Congressional delegates to propose independence ... Virginia publishes its Bill of Rights ... British at Fort Lee, N.J. ... Washington retreats to Pennsylvania, defeats Hessian troops at Trenton, New Jersey ... Benedict Arnold is defeated at Lake Champlain ... Congress retires to Baltimore ... William Howe, commander-in-chief of British army in America, takes New York and Rhode Island ... British, without trial, hang Nathan Hale as spy ... British defeat small colonial fleet on Lake Champlain ... Patriots attack British ships off Georgia ... Congress (March 15, 1776) resolves that authority of British Crown be suppressed ... British drive American troops from Canada, but Washington forces British to give up Boston (March 17, 1776) ... Britain recruits Hessian mercenaries for American war (August, 1776) ... Congress retires to Baltimore ... Thomas Paine publishes *Common Sense* (January 10, 1776), first important demand for independence ... South Carolina creates constitution, foreshadowing independent governments in colonies ... British defeat rebels at naval battle off Block Island ... Halifax Resolves (April 12, 1776): Provincial Congress at Halifax, North Carolina, instructs its delegates to stand for independence ... Congress (May 15, 1776) recommends that all colonies establish their own governments "sufficient to the exigencies of their affairs." ... Rhode Island publicly announces independence (May 4, 1776) ... Patriot gunners fight off British attack in South Carolina (late June, 1776) ... Local patriot militia drives off British flotilla attempting to seize St. George's, Maryland island near mouth of Potomac River ...

British Admiral Richard Howe arrives off Staten Island with 11,000 soldiers and more than 100 ships. (July 12, 1776) ... British warships sail to Tappan Zee on Hudson River, demonstrating weakness of American defense ... Washington's

army winters at Morristown, New Jersey ... British General Howe's force stands at about 30,000 men ... Revolutionaries defeat British at Princeton, New Jersey ... British capture Fort Morris, in Sunbury, Georgia ... Americans launch warships *Warren* and *Providence*, at Providence, Rhode Island (April 15, 1776) ... Rhode Island declares independence (May 4, 1776) ... Pennsylvania ships force British to withdraw on Delaware River ... John Paul Jones takes command of *Providence* ... Benedict Arnold fights rearguard action against British, in Canada ... Americans end attempt to take Canada (June 24, 1776) ... Regular British forces end operations in the Carolinas for two years ... British occupy Staten Island, New York (June 30, 1776) ... New Jersey adopts Constitution (July 2, 1776) ... Revolutionary

forces defeat British General John Burgoyne at Saratoga, New York, ending British plan to split colonies along Hudson River ... British forces defeat Washington in Pennsylvania ... Washington orders his troops to be inoculated against smallpox (1777) ... Washington in winter quarters at Valley Forge, Pa ... British evacuate Philadelphia, fearing French-fleet blockade ... British capture Savannah, Georgia ... Americans defeat British, at Stony Point, New York ... British capture Charleston, overrun South Carolina ... British consider kidnapping Martha Washington. The Declaration of Independence is read to Washington's troops, in New York City ... Patriots recapture Elizabethtown, New Jersey ... Benedict Arnold, traitor to U.S. cause, commands British against rebels in Richmond, Va ... Provincial Congress in New York formally adopts Declaration of Independence, joining 12 other colonies ... Utmost joy greets public proclamation of Declaration of Independence ... Congressional delegates sign Declaration of Independence ... British invade Manhattan (Sept.15, 1776) ... Thomas Jefferson asserts Americans are not British subjects in open revolt against their own government but already a distinct entity unto themselves: independence is not sedition . . . Washington fears British capture of New York City and the North River, which links with the Hudson River, centers for north-south colonial commerce and communication . . . Fifteen British ships arrive in St. Lawrence River . . . British burn Portland, Maine . . . General Montgomery occupies Montreal . . . It takes nearly a week for news of the battles of Lexington and Concord to reach Philadelphia, nearly a month to get as far as South Carolina . . . Massachusetts Provincial Congress mobilizes 13,600 colonial soldiers . . . Popular vote rejects constitution drafted by Mass. Provincial Congress . . . British troops in Boston are reinforced . . . Mass. Governor imposes martial law . . . Joseph Warren, colonial general, is killed at Bunker Hill, Boston . . . General Washington travels 12 days, Philadelphia to Cambridge, Mass., to assume formal command of Continental Army of about 17,000 men . . . King George closes American colonies to trade and commerce (March 1, 1776) . . . New Hampshire adopts first state constitution (January 5, 1776) . . . American troops under Colonel Henry Knox arrive at Cambridge, Mass., with 43 British cannon and 16 mortars captured by Ethan Allen and Green Mountain Boys at Fort Ticonderoga . . . American troops reach Crown Point, New York, after rowing length of Lake Champlain . . . Patrick Henry is sworn as governor of Virginia . . . Congress learns that George III rejected "Olive

Branch" petition, declaring colonies in open state of rebellion (1775) . . . Jefferson claims that "Honor, justice, and humanity forbid us tamely to surrender that freedom which we received from our gallant ancestors, which our innocent posterity have a right to receive from us. We cannot endure the

infamy and guilt of resigning succeeding generations to that wretchedness which inevitably awaits them, if we basely entail hereditary bondage upon them. Our cause is just. Our internal resources are great; and, if necessary, foreign assistance is undoubtedly attainable. In our own native land, in

defense of the freedom that is our birthright and which we ever enjoyed until the late violation of it, for the protection of our property acquired solely by the honest industry of our forefathers and ourselves, against violence actually offered, we have taken up arms. We shall lay them down when hostilities shall cease on the part of the aggressors and all danger of their being renewed shall be removed, and not before." . . . French minister suggests to Spain that Spain join France in secret aid to Britain's American colonies . . . Congress votes to open American ports to all nations except Britain (April, 1776) . . . Peace conference, on Staten Island (Sept., 1776), fails when colonists refuse to revoke Declaration of Independence before discussion can begin . . . Washington recrosses Delaware River (late December, 1776), surprises Hessian garrison at Trenton, New Jersey . . . Congress gives Washington dictatorial powers, flees Philadelphia for Baltimore . . . Washington eludes British force under General Cornwallis, near Trenton, New Jersey, inflicts heavy casualties on the British at Princeton . . . Victories vastly improve American morale . . . First foreign recognition of United States flag (February, 1778) . . . British defeat rebels under General Israel Putnam at Horseneck Land, Ct. . . . British cop Peekskill, New York . . . Patriot militia slaughter Indians at Gnadenhutten, Ohio . . . Tories and Indians under Indian chief, Joseph Brant, raid Minisink, New York . . . Continental Congress ratifies French alliance . . . Patriots under John Paul Jones raid Whitehaven, in northwest England . . . Benedict Arnold leads Patriot raid on St. Johns, Canada . . . Second Continental Congress resolves to hold Fort Ticonderoga and Crown Point . . . Patriots under Benedict Arnold re-enter Philadelphia . . . British declare martial law in Canada . . . Spain declares war on Great Britain (late June, 1779) . . . The name "United States of America" is officially first used (July 11, 1778) . . . British burn Georgetown, South Carolina . . . British destroy Norwalk, CT. . . . Continental Congress commissions the Frenchman Marquis de Lafayette a U.S. major general . . . British General Carleton, after his Lake Champlain triumph, abandons plans to invade American colonies from the north . . . British force occupies Newport, R.I., naval base . . . Congress authorizes privateering raids on British shipping, and suggests loyalist American colonists be disarmed . . . American and French armies march through Philadelphia (Sept. 2, 1781) . . . New York City burns (Sept. 21, 1776) . . . Lancaster, Pa., new capital of U.S. (Sept. 27, 1777) . . . John Paul Jones captures two British ships . . . British evacuate Rhode Island . . . York, Pa., becomes capital of U.S. (Sept. 30, 1777) . . . General Washington directs American-French siege of British in Yorktown, Va. . . British leave Charleston, South Carolina . . . David Bushnell invents one-man, egg-shaped, wooden submarine, *American Turtle* . . . Congress dispatches force against Indians in Wyoming Valley, in eastern Pennsylvania, (1778) . . . British open peace talks with Benjamin Franklin in Paris!

The Paris Peace Treaty

The Paris Peace Treaty ended America's Revolutionary War. Five years after declaring independence, the Americas beat the British on the battlefield: The British surrendered to General George Washington, at Yorktown, Virginia, in October 1781. In the peace treaty, (September 1783), England acknowledged the independence of its thirteen former colonies in North America—the United States of America. The U.S.'s northern boundary was fixed at approximately where it is today. The Mississippi River was the western boundary. Spanish Florida was the southern border. In 1787, delegates from twelve of the thirteen states (stubborn Rhode Island chose not to be present) composed four prescient parchment pages protecting Americans in their beliefs, thoughts, emotions, and sensations—the Constitution of the United States, a bundle of com-

promises that works. The Constitution created a strong central government. Thousands of amendments have been proposed; twenty-seven have been ratified by the states. The first ten amendments are the Bill of Rights. The source of all political power in the United States is We the People.

The Paris Peace Treaty (1783)

...ART. I.—His Britannic Majesty... *acknowledges the said United States, viz. New Hampshire, Massachusetts Bay, Rhode Island, and Providence Plantations, Connecticut, New York, New Jersey, Pennsylvania, Delaware, Maryland, Virginia, North Carolina, South Carolina, and Georgia, to be free, sovereign and independent States; that he treats with them as such, and for himself, his heirs and successors, relinquishes all claims to the Government, proprietary and territorial rights of the same, and every part thereof.*

ART. II.—*And that all disputes which might arise in future, on the subject of the boundaries of the said United States may be prevented, it is hereby agreed and declared, that the following are, and shall be their boundaries, viz.: From the northwest angle of Nova Scotia, viz.: that angle which is formed by a line drawn due north from the source of Saint Croix River to the Highlands; along the said Highlands which divide those rivers that empty themselves into the river St. Lawrence, from those which fall into the Atlantic Ocean, to the northwesternmost head of Connecticut River; thence down along the middle of that river, to the forty-fifth degree of north latitude; from thence, by a line due west on said latitude, until it strikes the river Iroquois or Cataraquy; thence along the middle of said river into Lake Ontario, through the middle of said lake until it strikes the communication by water between that lake and Lake Erie; thence along the middle of said communication into Lake Erie, through the middle of said lake until it arrives at the water communication between that lake and Lake Huron; thence along the middle of said water communication into the Lake Huron; thence through the middle of said lake to the water communication between that lake and Lake Superior; thence through Lake Superior northward of the Isles Royal and Phelipeaux, to the Long Lake; thence through the middle of said Long Lake, and the water communication between it and the Lake of the Woods, to the said Lake of the Woods; thence through the said lake to the most northwestern point thereof, and from thence on a due west course to the river Mississippi; thence by a line to be drawn along the* middle of the said river Mississippi until it shall intersect the northernmost part of the thirty-first degree of north latitude. South, by a line to be drawn due east from the determination of the line last mentioned, in the latitude of thirty-one degrees north of the Equator, to the middle of the river Appalachicola or Catahouche; thence along the middle thereof to its junction with the Flint River; thence straight to the head of St. Mary's River; and thence down along the middle of St. Mary's River to the Atlantic Ocean. East, by a line to be drawn along the middle of the river St. Croix, from its mouth in the Bay of Fundy to its source, and from its source directly north to the aforesaid Highlands, which divide the rivers that fall into the Atlantic Ocean from those which fall into the river St. Lawrence; comprehending all islands within twenty leagues of any part of the shores of the United States, and lying between lines to be drawn due east from the points where the aforesaid boundaries between Nova Scotia on the one part, and East Florida on the other, shall respectively touch the Bay of Fundy and the Atlantic Ocean; excepting such islands as now are, or heretofore have been, within the limits of the said province of Nova Scotia.

"Though I act wrong in most things, I have too much spirit to accept the crown and be a cipher."—King George III, two years before he became king. Later, he said about the American revolt: "I am not sorry that blows must decide."

ART. III.—It is agreed that the people of the United States shall continue to enjoy unmolested the right to take fish of every kind on the Grand Bank, and on all the other banks of Newfoundland; also in the Gulph of Saint Lawrence, and at all other places in the sea where the inhabitants of both countries used at any time heretofore to fish. And also that the inhabitants of the United States shall have liberty to take fish of every kind on such part of the coast of Newfoundland as British fishermen shall use (but not to dry or cure the same on that island) and also on the coasts, bays and creeks of all other of His Britannic Majesty's dominions in America; and that the American fishermen shall have liberty to dry and cure fish in any of the unsettled bays, harbours and creeks of Nova Scotia, Magdalen Islands, and Labrador, so long as the same shall remain unsettled; but so soon as the same or either of them shall be settled, it shall not be lawful for the said fishermen to dry or cure fish at such settlements, without a previous agreement for that purpose with the inhabitants, proprietors or possessors of the ground.

Art. IV.—It is agreed that creditors on either side shall meet with no lawful impediment to the recovery of the full value in sterling money, of all *bona fide* debts heretofore contracted.

Art. V.—It is agreed that the Congress shall earnestly recommend it to the legislatures of the respective States, to provide for the restitution of all estates, rights and properties which have been confiscated, belonging to real British subjects, and also of the estates, rights and properties of persons resident in districts in the possession of His Majesty's arms, and who have not borne arms against the said United States. And that persons of any other description shall have free liberty to go to any part or parts of any of the thirteen United States, and therein to remain twelve months, unmolested in their endeavours to obtain the restitution of such of their estates, rights and properties as may have been confiscated; and that Congress shall also earnestly recommend to the several States a reconsideration and revision of all acts or laws regarding the premises, so as to render the said laws or acts perfectly consistent, not only with justice and equity, but with that spirit of conciliation which, on the return of the blessings of peace, should universally prevail. And that Congress shall also earnestly recommend to the several States, that the estates, rights and properties of such last mentioned persons, shall be restored to them, they refunding to any persons who may be now in possession, the *bona fide* price (where any has been given) which such persons may have paid on purchasing any of the said lands, rights or properties, since the confiscation. And it is agreed, that all persons who have any interest in confiscated lands, either by debts, marriage settlements or otherwise, shall meet with no lawful impediment in the prosecution of their just rights.

Art. VI.—That there shall be no future confiscations made, nor any prosecutions commenced against any person or persons for, or by reason of the part which he or they may have taken in the present war; and that no person shall, on that account, suffer any future loss or damage, either in his person, liberty, or property; and that those who may be in confinement on such charges, at the time of the ratification of the treaty in America, shall be immediately set at liberty, and the prosecutions so commenced be discontinued.

Art. VII.—There shall be a firm and perpetual peace between His Britannic Majesty and the said States, and between the subjects of the one and the citizens of the other, wherefore all hostilities, both by sea and land, shall from henceforth cease; All prisoners on both sides shall be set at liberty, and His Britannic Majesty shall, with all convenient speed, and without causing any destruction, or carrying away any negroes or other property of the American inhabitants, withdraw all his armies, garrisons and fleets from the said United States, and from every post, place and harbour within the same; leaving in all fortifications the American artillery that may be therein; And shall also order and cause all archives, records, deeds and papers, belonging to any of the said States, or their citizens, which, in the course of the war, may have fallen into the hands of his officers, to be forthwith restored and deliver'd to the proper States and persons to whom they belong.

Art. VIII.—The navigation of the river Mississippi, from its source to the ocean, shall forever remain free and open to the subjects of Great Britain, and the citizens of the United States.

Art. IX.—In case it should so happen that any place or territory belonging to Great Britain or to the United States, should have been conquer'd by the arms of either from the other, before the arrival of the said provisional articles in America, it is agreed, that the same shall be restored without difficulty, and without requiring any compensation. . . .

* * *

"The glittering and sounding generalities of natural right (which) make up the Declaration of Independence."

—RUFUS CHOATE

* * *

"Yesterday, the greatest question was decided which ever was debated in America, and a greater perhaps never was nor will be decided among men. A resolution was passed without one dissenting colony, 'that these United Colonies are, and of right ought to be, free and independent States.' "

—JOHN ADAMS

* * *

"I have never had a feeling, politically, that did not spring from the sentiments embodied in the Declaration of Independence. . . . I have often inquired of myself what great principle or idea it was that kept this Confederacy so long together. It was not the mere matter of separation of the colonies from the motherland, but that sentiment in the Declaration of Independence which gave liberty not alone to the people of this country, but hope to all the world, for all future time. It was that which gave promise that in due time the weights would be lifted from the shoulders of all men, and that should have an equal chance. This is the sentiment embodied in the Declaration of Independence. . . . I would rather be assassinated on this spot than surrender it."

—ABRAHAM LINCOLN

* * *

"Hail! Independence, hail! Heaven's next best gift."

—JAMES THOMSON

Concord Hymn

In 1837, Ralph Waldo Emerson composed the Concord Hymn:

"By the rude bridge that arched the flood,
Their flag to April's breeze unfurled,
Here once the embattled farmers stood,
and fired the shot heard 'round the world."